Deterrence in the 21st Century

Editor

MAX G. MANWARING

*(Professor of Military Strategy,
US Army War College)*

FRANK CASS
LONDON • PORTLAND, OR

First published in 2001 in Great Britain by
FRANK CASS AND COMPANY LIMITED
Newbury House,
900 Eastern Avenue,
London IG2 7HH, England

and in the United States of America by
FRANK CASS
c/o ISBS
5824 N.E. Hassalo Street,
Portland, Oregon 97213-3644

Copyright © 2001 Frank Cass & Co. Ltd

Website: *www.frankcass.com*

British Library Cataloguing in Publication Data

Deterrence in the 21st century
1. Deterrence (Strategy)
I. Manwaring, Max G.
355'.0217

ISBN 0 7146 5133 8 (cloth)
ISBN 0 7146 8160 1 (paper)

Library of Congress Cataloging-in-Publication Data

Deterrance in the 21st century / editor Max G. Manwaring.
p. cm.
Includes bibliographical references and index.
ISBN 0-7146-5133-8 (cloth) – ISBN 0-7146-8160-1 (pbk.)
1. Deterrance (Strategy). 2. United States – Military policy.
I. Manwaring, Max G.

U162.6 .D485 2000
355'.033073 – dc21   00-064373

This group of studies first appeared in a Special Issue on 'Deterrence in the 21st Century' of
Small Wars & Insurgencies (ISSN 0956-2318) 11/2 (Autumn 1999)
published by Frank Cass

Printed in Great Britain by
Anthony Rowe Ltd., Chippenham, Wilts.

Deterrence in the 21st Century

Also in this series

Contents

Editor's Preface

MAX G. MANWARING

This special edition of *Small Wars & Insurgencies* stems from a symposium conducted in December 1999 by the Center for Strategic Leadership at the US Army War College in Carlisle, Pennsylvania. The symposium addressed 'Deterrence in the 21st Century,' and provided a practitioner's overview of deterrence policy and strategy, and the contemporary challenges they face. Although this volume is based on the symposium, it is not a comprehensive record of the proceedings. Rather, it is organized as an anthology of the 'best of the best' presentations – revised in the light of the discussions that took place at the symposium – and complemented by two chapters that fill important gaps in the limited dialogue. The primary conclusions of the symposium, and the driving concepts behind this compendium, are that it is imperative to reopen and broaden the deterrence debate, and to – hopefully – provide an impetus for policy change.

Since the ending of the Cold War, strategic concerns have played little part in the debate as to what to do with the billions of dollars allocated to national and global security. The general result, in the United States, has been the *ad hoc* and piecemeal crisis management of security affairs. That approach, in turn, has lead to *ad hoc*, piecemeal, and less-than-desirable results – and high personnel, monetary, and political costs. It must be remembered that, if one wants to optimize efficiency or effectiveness, one must precede reform, structure, and budget considerations with clear policy direction – and a strategy and organizational structure that defines how to achieve it.

Panelists, discussants, and participants sketched the problems and threats of the post-Cold War strategic environment, and argued that deterring the complex and diverse threats in that environment requires a new policy and strategy. The intent was to establish that contemporary deterrence demands replacing the old 'nuclear theology' with broad, integrated, and long-term culturally-oriented approaches. These approaches would confront better the myriad state and non-state, nuclear and non-nuclear, conventional and non-conventional, military and non-military, and asymmetric threats that have heretofore been ignored or wished away.

Separately and collectively, the contributors to this anthology focus on that challenge. At the same time, they do essentially what 'Mr X' did in his 1947 *Foreign Affairs* article entitled 'The Sources of Soviet Conduct'.[1] They examine the threat situation in the contemporary global security arena. They analyze specific problems of deterrence and strategy. They outline cogent issues. They implicitly and explicitly come to grips with the lessons that should have been learned over the past several years. They establish the beginning underpinnings of a deterrence theory of engagement to manage the contemporary environment and associated threats. And, lastly, they take the discussion of deterrence out of the 'TOP SECRET' realm and begin to publicly educate decision-makers, policy-makers, opinion-makers, and the citizenry regarding the realistic requirements for contemporary national and global security.

As a consequence, decision-makers, policy-makers, opinion-makers, and their staffs should be able to develop a national security blueprint to confront more effectively the diverse threats of the 21st century. That is to say, leaders with this kind of information should be able to do what was done after the publication of 'Sources of Soviet Conduct.' Over a period of time, debate, symposia and conferences, and gaming elaborated and refined the conceptual, organizational, and operational elements that were proposed by Mr X (George F. Kennan) and promulgated in NSC-68, and that laid the foundations for the US Cold War policy of 'containment'.

This anthology, then, commends itself to the reader to provoke thought about what governments and international organizations ought to do when faced with the 'new world disorder'. In these terms, it suggests what citizens in the global community ought to demand of their governments and that community. Thus, we commend this volume to you – the reader – with the hope that you will make effective use of the insights of the contributors.

For the most part, the contributors are not scholars. The individual contributors are, as former US National Security Advisor Brent Scowcroft, has observed, 'Knowledgeable and experienced, and have proven track records in the only arena that counts – actually dealing with the problems they discuss.'[2] Thus, we wish to thank the contributors whose knowledge, experience, analytical powers, wisdom, and many hours of work made this book possible. We also wish to respectfully dedicate this volume to General John R. Galvin, US Army (Ret.). This anthology is part of a continuing effort to revitalize strategic thinking as it pertains to 'uncomfortable' contemporary conflicts. It evolved from General Galvin's call for a new paradigm to fight the most prevalent and most likely forms of conflict in the world today.[3]

Finally, neither this compendium nor the individual studies in it should be construed as reflecting the official positions of the US government, the Department of Defense, or the Department of State. Contributors, alone are responsible for any errors of fact or judgment.

NOTES

1. X (George F. Kennan), 'The Sources of Soviet Conduct', *Foreign Affairs* (July 1947) pp. 566–82.
2. Interviews.
3. General John R. Galvin, 'Uncomfortable Wars: Toward a New Paradigm', *Parameters* (Dec. 1986) pp. 2–8.

Introduction

WILLIAM J. CROWE JR

When the Chinese say, 'May you live in interesting times', I think they had in mind a period such as we are experiencing right now. I wrote in my book, *The Line of Fire*, that I sometimes regretted that my military professional life was shaped by a single global factor: the challenge of the Soviet Union, which was constantly in the forefront of our minds as our one formidable military adversary. Those times certainly were not uninteresting, but the current global situation is even more intellectually diverse and challenging. My post-military life has deepened and widened the already broad world perspective I had acquired as Chairman of the Joint Chiefs of Staff, as a unified area commander, as a naval officer in other military assignments, and as chairman of the President's Foreign Intelligence Advisory Board (PFIAB). This was followed by 3½ years as US ambassador to the Court of Saint James's, London.

As Max Manwaring and the various contributors to this timely deterrence collection suggest, our world is truly in flux. It is moving so rapidly that perspectives, goals, and strategies that seemed appropriate a few years after the end of the Cold War are continuously being rethought and reshaped.

Certainly the global picture has altered dramatically in an extremely short time, and continues to change rapidly. In essence we are witnessing firsthand one of the great watersheds of history. We are actually experiencing it and reading about it in our newspapers and seeing it on our television sets. We saw the edifice of communism shatter, the Soviet Empire crumble, and now throughout much of the world, people are throwing off their shackles and moving – in a very halting and uncertain way – toward pluralism and free markets.

As Americans we applaud these developments. At the same time, we are aware that our future is not necessarily secure and assured. I submit that we are in for a protracted period of uncertainty and struggle. The current transitions are bringing new pockets of poverty and new pockets of wealth, with a widening divergence between the two. New governments have in several cases fashioned important improvements through economic liberalization and greater individual freedom, but the international community will still suffer a great deal of confusion, trauma, frustration, and disillusionment before the new world order sorts itself out. And, although each nation and each people must be responsible for their own actions, the United States – as the free world leader and as the remaining superpower – will undoubtedly be deeply involved in the global revolution.

We live in an international community with no prominent adversary. Third World threats, although real, are more ephemeral, individually less dangerous in the short term (although not so cumulatively), and not especially predictable. Without the consuming confrontation between two armed camps, not every crisis or every challenge requires American reaction or intervention. Washington's primary international problem now is to determine when our interests are genuinely at risk and what their relative priorities are – in other words, to be selective as to our involvement. Unfortunately, this is a perplexing task, and our republican system of government has difficulty in coping with ambiguous, 'low-intensity' political-military conflicts.

Such challenges abound. In many parts of the world traditional enmities grounded in ethnic feuds and national rivalries are thriving, and such rivalries have the capacity to blossom into wider challenges. The doomsday anxieties that so deeply marked the collective psyche of the Cold War generation are not totally a thing of the past. The possibility of several countries employing nuclear, chemical, or biological weapons of mass destruction on their neighbors is made more likely by proliferation. Witness the 1998 decisions of both India and Pakistan to set off nuclear devices. In a sense, the United States is being expected to act as an international policeman and conciliator for regional wars, to control rogue states, and to settle low-intensity conflicts. That is the burden of our role as the world's only superpower. Winston Churchill once commented: 'With great power comes great responsibility.'

This anthology argues that facing the diverse threats in the 'new world disorder' requires new attitudes and new approaches. I agree. Contemporary deterrence demands replacing the old 'nuclear theology' with more relevant strategy. For example, new policies are needed to deal with the myriad state, non-state, and trans-national nuclear and non-nuclear menaces that have heretofore been ignored or wished away.

The naïveté of arguing that the United States is the only superpower in the post-Cold War world – and has nothing to fear from any other political actor – is too simplistic and, on occasion, dangerous. The reality of such irresponsibility is that there are state and non-state actors that have the potential to threaten US interests and global well-being. Thus, it is incumbent on individual powers and the international community to understand and cope with the threats imposed by contemporary chaos.

The intent of General Michael Carns and Professor Colin Gray in Part One of this work is to reexamine the broad concept of deterrence as it applies to the 'Russian Bear, Asian Dragons, and 1,000 Snakes'. In turn, it argues the need for a new and broader deterrence policy that can and will respond to the diverse 'non-military' threats looming on the not-too-distant horizon. In that context, Part Two analyzes a series of troubling issues – from 'Some Possible Surprises in Our Nuclear Future,' to questions of deterrence and defense in a biological and chemical environment, in addition to terrorism and information warfare – that make the case for a host of changes.

Finally, in Part Three, Dr Max Manwaring and Ambassador Edwin Corr provide some strategic level ideas regarding possible new deterrence policies and political-military responses.

These writings will, hopefully, encourage the process of rethinking both problems and reactions. The editor and contributors to this anthology should be commended for this impressive effort. It should be required reading for scholars, policy-makers, diplomats, soldiers, and other leaders who must plan for, fight, or otherwise attempt to manage conflict in the new global security environment.

Part One

Setting the Stage for a Discussion of Deterrence

Reopening the Deterrence Debate: Thinking about a Peaceful and Prosperous Tomorrow

MICHAEL P. C. CARNS

Since the end of the Cold War, the nature of the global security system and the verities that shaped US purposes, policies, and priorities have undergone fundamental changes. Cold War concepts of security and deterrence are no longer completely relevant. We are in a new global security environment that involves the integration of free markets, technologies, and countries to a degree never before witnessed. The growling, nuclear-armed Soviet bear was relatively easy to understand and deal with. What is not easy to understand and respond to are the many 'smaller' threats – and opportunities – that stem from global integration. Yet, as the country that benefits most from global integration, the US has a pressing national interest in maintaining and enhancing the new order.

The New Strategic Environment

When what mattered most were military bases, preserving access to sea lines of communication, chokepoints, and raw materials – and denying those assets to the Soviet Union and its surrogates – the US could generally ignore internal conditions in other countries. But, since the US is now also interested in the need for non-hostile dispositions toward the country, the non-proliferation of weapons of mass destruction, the capacity of other countries to buy American-made products, the continued development of democratic and free market institutions, and human rights – as well as cooperation on shared problems such as illegal drugs, the environment, and the victims of natural and man-made disasters – then the US must concern itself with the causes and consequences of regional and national instability.

The 'unstable peace' and chaos of the post-Cold War era are caused by myriad instabilities. The causes include increasing poverty, human starvation, widespread disease, and lack of political and socio-economic justice. The consequences are seen in such forms as social violence, criminal anarchy, refugee flows, illegal drug trafficking and organized crime, extreme nationalism, irredentism, religious fundamentalism, insurgency, ethnic cleansing, and environmental devastation. These conditions tend to be exploited by militant nationalists, militant reformers, ideologues, demagogues, civil and military bureaucrats, terrorists, insurgents, warlords, and rogue states for their own narrow purposes. As a result, in the words of Leslie Gelb, the interdependent global community is experiencing 'wars of national debilitation, a steady run of uncivil wars sundering fragile but functioning nation states and gnawing at the well-being of stable nations'.

In the chaos of the 'new world disorder', the threat of devastating attacks on the US, its interests, and its friends perpetrated by the former Soviet Union, China, and other nuclear powers retains a certain credibility. At the same time, the challenges for contemporary security and deterrence policy will intensify with the growing sophistication of biological and chemical war, and cyber war. These challenges to deterrence policy will be gravely complicated by 'non-traditional' threats and menaces emanating from rogue states, sub-state and trans-national terrorists, insurgents, illegal drug traffickers, organized criminals, warlords, militant fundamentalists, ethnic cleansers, and 1,000 other 'snakes' with a cause – and the will to conduct asymmetrical warfare.

In this security environment, the US has little choice but to reexamine and rethink security and deterrence as they apply to the various state, non-state, and trans-national nuclear and non-nuclear threats and menaces that have heretofore been ignored or wished away. As Thomas Friedman has suggested, the US cannot expect the 'hidden hand' of the free market to work without a 'hidden fist'. That is to say, 'McDonald's cannot flourish without McDonald Douglas. The hidden fist that keeps the world safe for Silicon Valley technologies is called the United States Army, Air Force, Navy, and Marine Corps.'

To help sustain and continue to benefit from the new globalization, the US must take the responsibility to lead, control, and manage the negative consequences of global integration. As was the case in determining how to 'contain' a hegemonic Soviet bear, the first step would be to craft a carefully thought-out, holistic, long-term, and phased national security policy that deters – or at least manages – existing and emergent threats. This is important not only because the promise is great, but also because the alternative is unacceptable.

Deterrence: The Art of the Possible

To understand precisely what it is we are talking about, a few fundamentals are essential.

First, and most important, deterrence is the attempt to influence how and what an enemy thinks and does. That is, deterrence is a state of mind that – hopefully – prevents a deterree from acting in a way a deterrer considers harmful. Thus, the deterrence 'rule of thumb' is to determine precisely what a hostile leadership values most and identify exactly how that cultural 'thing' – whatever it is – might be held at risk. At the same time, the deterrence rule of thumb must also consider – as opposed to the proverbial 'stick' – what 'carrots' might be offered as deterrents. In these terms, deterrence can work only if the intended deterree chooses to be deterred. The problem, by definition, is that conflict and the strategy to pursue or prevent it is a dialogue between two or more independent wills. As a consequence, probably the single most important dimension of a deterrence strategy is clarity of communication between culturally different deterrers and deterees.

In this context, a successful deterrence policy and strategy must recognize that one deterrent or another may fail. The possibility of failure leads to other requirements. As examples, beyond unilateral US military reaction, there are the ideas of enhancing collective security measures, the possibility of going to other already proven and ageless security measures, and the notion of developing 'new' means of deterrence. Thus, deterrence must also address the relationship with the other concepts such as traditional and non-traditional compellance, dissuasion, defense, and denial – and how to integrate these ideas into policy, strategy, doctrine, and operations with respect to old, new, and emerging adversaries.

Deterrence, then, should not be reduced to a single dominant aspect. Success cannot be guaranteed by buying more or better nuclear forces, conventional and unconventional military forces, superior intelligence, genius in command, or relative morality. Success will be the result of a unified, coherent, long-term, and culturally-oriented policy and strategy that integrates all the civil and military elements of US national power synergistically to influence the behavior of diverse possible adversaries.

The Russian Bear, Asian Dragons, and other Nuclear Powers

It is a paradox of the present global security environment that at a time when powerful forces in the US have argued that America is the only superpower in the contemporary world – and has nothing to fear from any other global political actor – some actors are in fact actively acquiring nuclear weapons for potential use against the US and its interests. These actors range from Russia to China, North Korea, India, and Pakistan to Iran, Israel, and even South Africa. Then, there are those countries such as Brazil who could develop their own nuclear capabilities very soon after a political decision was made to do so. In all, it is arguable that a fresh policy framework is called for to manage the evolution of twenty-first century power relationships. Success in doing so depends on applying innovative perspectives, coupled with vigorous and enlightened US leadership.

Russia

The Russian nuclear threat is well documented in the media and in international arms control agreements. Nevertheless, it is important to review some fundamental issues regarding Russian nuclear deterrence policy and strategy. For a variety of reasons, we may wish to ignore or cleverly 'spin' what the Russian leadership says about the US and how they see the world. If we do, however, we may well forgo opportunities to manage a better relationship, and we do so at our own peril. If we place any credence in what its political and military leaders are saying, Russia considers the US to be a threat to international stability and – more directly – a threat to its own national security. They have said this from former-President Yeltsin on down. They have been saying so for several years and on numerous occasions – over NATO enlargement, over Bosnia, over Kosovo, and over Chechnya.

In November 1999, Defense Minister Marshal Igor Sergeyev publicly accused the US of 'seeking to establish control over the North Caucasus' by playing the Afghan card in Chechnya. Sergeyev's argument is the US and NATO are trying to weaken Russia by all means, including the 'the use of force, disregard for the norms of international law, and *diktat* and high-handedness'. Also, recently, the Chief of the Russian General Staff suggested that Moscow could expect NATO to use force against former Soviet territory, just as it had in Iraq. In this context, he and others have almost proudly noted the conduct of Russian missile, submarine, and aircraft exercises that to many appear to be patterned after Cold War activities.

More disturbing than the words we are hearing is the turbulence and the growing dysfunctioning of the Russian government. Even among those who discount what Russian leaders are saying, most would agree that the strategic uncertainties regarding Russian internal instability are staggering. Few would venture to guess where Russia will be politically in five years – or even one year. Yet, most would predict that, even with resource limitations, Russia will continue to possess a large nuclear stockpile. It appears, then, that Russia intends to rely on its nuclear arsenal for at least the next decade as the primary means to ensure its security. Indicative of this greater reliance on nuclear weapons for both defense planning and declaratory policy is the recent announcement of an across-the-board increase in research and development as well as a start of production of new mobile 'tactical' weapons.

In sum, Russia is doing what it can to maintain as much nuclear capability as it can. It is expending very scarce resources on deploying a new mobile missile, keeping heavy multiple independent re-entry vehicle (MIRVed) missiles in the field, and retaining a massive infrastructure and the capability to produce new warheads. These developments are serious, indeed, and it is time for the US to think through the issue in an effort to manage the Russian relationship in such a manner as to sustain a hard-won peace.

China

Unlike Russia, China is an emerging power. Here again, the best we can do is note what Chinese leaders are saying, as well as what they are doing.

First, even more forcefully than in Russia, the Chinese are declaring the US to be a threat to their national security and to global security. It is argued that the US 1998 bombing of the pharmaceutical factory in Sudan was an act of state terrorism; that the 1999 bombing in the former Yugoslavia was an overt illegal act of aggression against a sovereign state; and that the bombing of the Chinese embassy in Belgrade was a war crime.

Second, in terms of behavior, it appears that the Chinese have made a long-term commitment to improve their nuclear capabilities. As examples, the acquisition of MIRV and solid fuel technologies, the deployment of increasingly longer-range mobile missiles, the announcement of the development of neutron warheads, the construction of a new strategic submarine to carry long-range missiles, and firing ballistic missiles near Taiwan indicate a determination to develop and deploy a robust nuclear arsenal.

Finally, it is argued that Americans should be concerned about Chinese nuclear modernization because soon they will be able to target all major US population centers.

These are sobering developments. As with Russia, it is time to reconsider the issue of Chinese deterrence in light of changing conditions and the need to manage correctly global power relationships. The fundamentals of deterrence, however, have not changed. Effective deterrence continues to depend on both real, not virtual, capabilities, and the perception of US resolve to respond against something of high value.

Other Emerging Nuclear Powers

Moving on to the next category of states that we must consider in a deterrence context, there is a consensus that about two dozen countries including North Korea, Iraq, and Iran – those that the State Department refers to as 'rogues' – represent a growing threat. These states, as does Russia, define the US as the enemy without any subtlety or reservation.

They believe, quite correctly it is hoped, that we are the major barrier in the way of their strategic territorial, political, religious, and personal goals. As a rule, these states are more risk prone than was the former Soviet Union. As an example, Iran fired the Shahab 3, with a range of some 1,300 kilometers, and further indicated that it was developing a Shahab 4, with an estimated range of at least 2,000 kilometers.

At the same time, North Korea tested a multi-stage missile – the Taepo Dong 1 – in the summer of 1998. It over-flew Japan, splashed down in the Pacific Ocean, and convinced several vulnerable countries that North Korea must be considered a serious threat to stability and peace all along the Asian Rim. North Korea is also reportedly working on a Taepo Dong 2 that might be capable of striking the continental US with a nuclear-weapons-size payload. As Keith Payne has pointed out, the conditions that we always valued in our Cold War deterrent relationship are not likely to pertain with North Korea and other new nuclear powers. Additionally, 'rogue' states see as their task deterring the US from intervening in their regions. As a consequence, deterrence is a proverbial two-way street – and in this case, the symmetry of the East–West relationship is absent.

Again, these developments are sufficiently threatening to require rethinking policy and strategy. In developing regional deterrent and defense strategies, understanding the regional and national military/political/cultural dynamics is critical to identifying those assets that should be held at risk for deterrent purposes. It is also essential to determine how best to communicate intentions, both with regard to public declaratory policy, as well as private communications and non-verbal messages to demonstrate resolve.

'The Poor Man's Nukes'

In addition to nuclear arms, weapons of mass destruction include cheap and accessible biological agents and man-made chemical compounds that attack the nervous system, skin, or blood. Biological and chemical weapons strikes could make whole regions of the world uninhabitable for long periods. Additionally, electronic (or cyber) warfare exposes enormous vital areas of national life to sabotage by virtually any computer 'hacker'. Such concerted sabotage could render a country, or part of it, unable to function. Given the low cost and virtually universal ease of access, it has been said that terrorists can order the poor man's nuclear bomb (chemical and biological weapons) from a catalog. Similarly, terrorists, or anyone else with the will, can find a computer hacker to create destruction and mayhem.

The hard evidence over time is that violence is all too often considered an acceptable option in attempting to achieve personal or institutional goals;

that non-state and even state actors prefer to resort to ambiguous and asymmetric forms of force to achieve their ends; and that 'only the foolish will fight fair'. For these reasons, the 'poor man's nuke' represents a growing and direct threat to US security and well-being, and to the ability of the US to use direct military force against ambiguous non-state targets as an instrument of that strategy.

There is a clear requirement to prepare and plan more comprehensively for the threat represented by the proliferation of weapons of mass destruction. In these terms, it cannot be assumed that the 'proven' logic of mutual assured destruction will apply in a regional, sub-state, organizational, or individual context. That is, regional states and messianic anti-Western zealots may well risk annihilation for outcomes Americans and other Westerners would consider 'irrational'. It would be wise for the US to think through these complex problems, case by case, before a conflict. Crisis management is not likely to suffice in the context of a multi-polar world in which one or a hundred 'irrational' actors are exerting differing types and levels of power.

Terrorists, Illegal Drug Traffickers, Other Organized Criminals, and 1,000 Other 'Snakes'

Current definitions of terrorism fail to capture the magnitude of the global threat. It has been defined as the sub-state application of violence or threatened violence intended to sow panic in a society, to weaken or even overthrow a given regime, and to bring about political change. It shades, sometimes, into insurgency and a substitute for conventional declared war between countries. The problem of sorting out an acceptable definition of terrorism is exacerbated by the development of hundreds of aggressive movements espousing varieties of nationalism, religious fundamentalism, fascism, and apocalyptic millenarianism – from Hindu nationalism in India to neo-fascism in Europe and the developing world to the example of the Branch Davidian cultism of Waco, Texas. Thus, the contemporary global community faces not one type of terrorism, but many. Importantly, terrorists, drug traffickers, organized criminals, and other 'snakes' are now significant global actors with the ability to compromise the integrity and sovereignty of individual nation states.

The common denominator seems to be that terrorists of all stripes have in fact become organized, highly trained paramilitary units who are conducting an offensive war campaign against a variety of nations and social systems. That war, of course, is not the conventional massing of uniformed armies in a given field. Rather, that campaign is conducted through both direct and indirect means. These means range from intimidation, corruption, and 'armed propaganda' to 'kneecapping', bombing discos, department stores, and large buildings to chemically and biologically poisoning subway systems, and to 'hacking' into the electronic storage, retrieval, analysis, and transmission of information and rendering a country unable to function.

Another common denominator of contemporary offensive terrorist war is the fact that nuclear, chemical, biological, and electronic 'weapons of mass destruction' are inexpensive and accessible – and easily transportable. All this leads well beyond terrorism, as we have known it. Walter Laqueur warns that 'Chances are that of 100 attempts at terrorist superviolence, 99 would fail. But the single successful one could claim many more victims, do more material damage, and unleash far greater panic than anything the world has yet experienced.'

Again, it is time to rethink both problem and response. New definitions and new terms have to be developed for new realities in order to develop a viable counter-terrorist offensive. The Italian experience during the late 1970s and early 1980s is instructive. In that case, Italian counter-terrorism planners understood that the situation was more than a complex law enforcement problem. It was agreed that the Red Brigades and the other 300 or more left and right-wing terrorist groups operating in Italy were dividing, corrupting, destabilizing, and destroying the Italian society as well as the government. Thus, terrorism, regardless of different internal ideological orientations, was identified as a national security problem.

The first step in the counter-terrorism process was to amend the Criminal Code and promulgate 'hard law' legislation directed specifically against terrorists. These foundational measures would facilitate an adequate response to the terrorist threat at the judicial, police, and intelligence levels. Next, it was recognized that an anti-terrorist strategy was a multi-dimensional series of 'wars within the war.' As only three examples, there was a 'legitimacy war,' an information 'war,' and of course a 'shooting' war. The government mobilized itself and the society to generate a powerful 'unity of effort' to plan and conduct those diverse wars, and to reestablish the kind of stability that is derived from popular perceptions that the authority of the state is genuine and effective – and that it uses morally correct means for reasonable and fair purposes. At a third level, there was a certain reluctance to take the broadened definition of national security to its logical conclusion and correspondingly broaden the role of the military to a controversial internal protection mission. Thus, the regular military took over generally routine, inconspicuous, and unobtrusive police functions to allow the State Police and the paramilitary *Carabinieri* freedom to concentrate on the anti-terrorism mission.

The point is that the Italians did not take up a defensive stance behind a facade of micro-level criminal sanctions designed to tighten airport security, impose trade sanctions against foreign companies that did business with nations that supported the Red Brigades and other terrorist factions, and deny visas to known terrorists. Rather, they made the decision to treat terrorism as a national security problem, and planned, organized, and implemented a unified political-economic-social-moral counter-offensive. As a result, it was only a matter of a year and a half to two years before the complex terrorist threat in Italy was brought under control.

The Ultimate Threat, the Challenge, and the Main Task for Now and the Future

A multi-polar world, in which one or a hundred actors are exerting differing types and levels of power within a set of cross-cutting alliances, appears to be more volatile and dangerous than the previous bipolar situation. Thus, it is incumbent on the US and the rest of the global community to understand and cope with the threats imposed by diverse state and non-state political players, think 'outside the box', and replace the old 'nuclear deterrence theology' with a broad strategy of deterrence as it applies to the 'Russian bear, Asian Dragons, and 1,000 snakes'.

The Ultimate Threat

The ultimate threat is that unless and until leaders at the highest levels recognize what is happening strategically, reorient thinking and actions appropriately, and are able to educate and lead their domestic publics into the realities of the post-Cold War world, it is only a matter of time before the destabilizing problems associated with global integration will mortally consume one vitally important actor or another. By then, it will probably be too late to exert decisive influence on the situation and political-military chaos, criminal anarchy, and 'teapot wars' will continue to spread. In the meantime, territory, infrastructure, and stability are quietly and slowly destroyed, and hundreds of thousands of innocents will continue to die.

The Challenge

The challenge, then, is to come to terms with the fact that contemporary security, at whatever level, is at its base a holistic political-diplomatic, socio-economic, psychological-moral, and military-police effort. The corollary is to change from a singular military-nuclear approach to a multi-dimensional, multi-organizational, and multi-cultural paradigm.

The Main Task

The task in the search for security now and for the future is to construct stability and well-being on the same strategic pillars that supported success and effectiveness in the past.

The first pillar of success is a conceptual requirement. That is, develop a realistic strategic vision, a philosophy, or theory of engagement. The second pillar is an organizational requirement. That is, the creation of a planning and management structure to establish as complete a unity of effort as possible to plan and implement the philosophy. The third is an organizational and operational requirement. Organizationally, it involves developing and implementing the appropriate combination of political, economic, informational, moral, and coercive instruments of national and international power to pursue the multi-dimensional requirements of the contemporary global security environment. Operationally, it involves learning to understand adversaries and potential adversaries culturally so as to influence their thought and behavior for US advantage.

These challenges and tasks are nothing radical. They are only basic security strategy and national and international asset management. By accepting these challenges and tasks, the US can help to replace conflict with cooperation and to harvest the hope and fulfill the promise that a new deterrence paradigm for a peaceful and prosperous tomorrow offers.

Deterrence and the Nature of Strategy

COLIN S. GRAY

Much as Britain's Royal Navy 'did' seapower for several centuries before Admiral Mahan discovered and popularized the concept, so deterrence actually has been 'done', certainly attempted, since strategic history began. There is a sense in which modern American defense policy and strategic studies created deterrence theory, but as George Quester, among others, reminded us many years ago, most certainly there was 'deterrence before Hiroshima'. The problem, of course, was that deterrence before Hiroshima probably demonstrated a poor track record of success. It would be unjust, and positively misleading, to argue that strategic history prior to 1945 is a record of the quite regular failure of deterrence. None the less, unjust and misleading (because oversimplified) or not, it is true that the history of wars, events which history has registered in abundance, is a history of deterrence failure. If Raymond Aron was correct in his judgment that 'prudence is the statesman's supreme virtue', then history has to be interpreted to show that many statesmen, at many times, at least when not facing nuclear-armed foes, believed that it was prudent to choose to go to war.

Deterrence often is discussed in terms that assign it an intrinsic moral quality. Of course, that is a nonsense. Bereft of detail about historical context, deterrence – even stable deterrence – order, and even peace, are necessarily neither desirable nor undesirable. Hitler's 'New Order' might have proved to be a lasting peace based upon conquest and the submission of foes. Deterrence is an admirable context in contrast to war, in the same way that peace is preferable to war. But, if the only peace on offer is the peace that rewards aggressors, then it would be unfortunate if potential resisters were deterred. My point is that even if we elect to discuss strategic ideas – in this case, deterrence – in fairly abstract terms, we need to remember that strategy inalienably is a practical subject pervaded with political meaning.

Because American political culture tends to be optimistic, forward-looking, and fairly eager to reward novelty, real or only apparent, the word 'new' is apt to trigger positive responses here. For an example not picked totally at random, to talk about 'new approaches' to deterrence suggests, certainly it implies, that new approaches are needed, and that new approaches will work better than old approaches. But, just what is it that is wrong with the allegedly old approaches? ('If it ain't broke, don't fix it!').

And, to risk some indecent exposure of evidence, or lack thereof, how well did the old approaches perform, and how do we know? These are perilously post-modern thoughts. Could it be that what we think we know about deterrence might be significantly wrong? No less to the point, might it be that the policy problem is not so much to devise bright and shiny 'new' approaches to the deterrence mission, but rather to reconsider the relative importance of that mission in the new security environment.

As befits a card-carrying academic, I shall attempt to penetrate to the heart of the matter here. What follows is an exercise in what we used to call 'policy science', which in this case means a policy-relevant analysis which examines the structure of a policy problem. Hence the ambitious and essentialist title of this paper, 'deterrence and the nature of strategy'.

The Argument

I would not risk insulting you by going 'back to basics' on definition of key concepts, were it not for the fact that both 'deterrence' and 'strategy' are abused regularly by many people who ought to know better. More to the point, such abuse really matters because the misuse of words may well reflect, and it must encourage, unsound thinking. Given that our ultimate practical referent here is war and peace, it seems to me to be downright irresponsible to tolerate concept abuse.

Adapting from Carl von Clausewitz, *strategy* is the use that is made of force and the threat of force for the ends of policy. Slight variation on that formula is acceptable, always provided strategy and strategic retain their core meaning of instrumentality. *Deterrence* refers to the effect when a person, institution, or polity decides not to take action that otherwise would have been taken, because of the belief or strong suspicion that intolerable consequences would ensue from such action. As *instrumentality* is key to strategy and strategic, so *effect* is critical to deterrence and deterrent. I apologize for advancing these sophomoric points, but the prevalence of error really is widespread.

For a glorious example of compound conceptual error, consider the term, 'the strategic deterrent'. The first of the two mortal sins committed in that phrase against sound thinking is the assertion that *any* military capability (or, indeed, anything else) inherently is deterring – '*the* deterrent'. The second sin is the claim that a particular military capability is distinctively strategic – 'the *strategic* deterrent'. To sum it all up, deterrence is a state of mind: it is a condition which is a chosen consequence of perception of threat, *among other factors*. Moreover, *all* military capabilities (*inter alia*), in use or in threat of use, have strategic meaning.

All forces are strategic forces. 'Strategic' does not mean important, independently and directly decisive, long-range, or nuclear. It means consequential for the course and outcome of conflicts.

All of this may strike you as a typical example of academic self-indulgence. You may be right. However, I believe I can show you why my insistence upon handling concepts with care really matters for practical issues in national and international security. Two illustrations of my point may suffice. For example, people in the mental habit of referring to long-range and nuclear-armed forces as *the deterrent*, are vulnerable to the erroneous belief that deterrence is secured by buying and maintaining incremental quantities of *the* great deterrent. After all, if those forces are known as *the* deterrent, you have settled preemptively by fiat what it is that purportedly deters. In Clintonspeak, 'it's *the* deterrent, stupid!' So, to secure more deterrence, we just need to buy more of *the* deterrent. One thousand nuclear-armed long-range missiles have to be twice as deterring as 500 such missiles, to hazard an essentialist case.

For another example in illustration of error, the virtue of strategy and war is affronted when we commit the solecism of talking about strategic forces. Such explicit and implicit 'strategic' demotion of the rest of the forces, those labelled non-strategic, is a mistake liable to promote poor planning and unsound policy. We need to think through the contributions that all kinds of armed forces, jointly and synergistically, make within what T. E. Lawrence (of Arabia fame) called 'the whole house of strategy', via the common currencies of military and then strategic effectiveness.

I am not suggesting that quantities of military capability are irrelevant for deterrent effect, and neither am I arguing that particular kinds of military power will not be more important than others in unique geostrategic and historical contexts. What I am saying is that neither strategy, nor deterrence as one of its instrumental consequences, reduces usefully to the simple treatment that I have been criticizing. These errors are not unrelated to the conceptual and consequential policy sins of the 1960s and 1970s, when some among us believed that so-called strategic weapons could be neatly divided into just two columns, the stabilizing and the destabilizing.

I have denounced any simple linearity in thought about deterrence. What I have tried to remind people is that while deterrence assuredly is keyed to acquisition of suitably fearsome military forces, you cannot in the partially non-linear reality of strategy just 'cut to the chase' by buying more of *the* deterrent. The core reason why that is so resides in the nature of strategy. I will now ignore usual scholarly practice, as well as the timeless rules of good storytelling, and reveal who the 'bad guy' is for the difficulties with deterrence. You may be less than startled to learn that, in my view, the challenge of deterrence is the challenge of good strategy. I am pleased to acknowledge my debt to an excellent essay published by Professor David Jablonsky in 1993, entitled 'Why Is Strategy Difficult?' The purpose of strategy, again following Clausewitz, is 'to impose our will on the enemy'. An enemy who chooses to be deterred is an enemy who chooses to subordinate his will to ours.

If you need to think prudently about deterrence, you have no intelligent choice other than to think prudently, which also means holistically, about strategy. Much of the nonsense that has been written by theorists and historians about deterrence in the nuclear era, flows quite directly from the fact that a lot of theory, defence analysis, and even nuanced efforts at narrative history, have not been well nested in a sound grasp of that 'whole house of strategy'.

There is a limit to how far I can take my thesis here. By way of narrative trajectory, this analysis now proceeds tersely to expose the bare bones of my argument. Subsequently, I develop the implication of the proposition that deterrence is difficult to do because strategy is difficult to do. This is not a counsel of despair, but it is a counsel of caution. *Caveat emptor*. If you buy a military machine because the sales brochure calls it *the great deterrent*, then more fool you.

What is Our Argument?

1. Deterrence is important, often is feasible, and is quite properly a concept with a high approval rating. (Of course, the deterrence that we approve of is our deterrence of others, not their deterrence of us. Remember that deterrence, like strategy, is an equal opportunity concept).

2. Though often, perhaps unusually, feasible, deterrence is *inherently* unreliable. Many claims made here are essentially contestable, but this one is not. Quite literally, deterrence can work only if the intended deterree chooses to be deterred. There is no way in which such a choice, for deterrence, can be guaranteed. The strategic world is significantly, though by no means entirely, non-linear. No matter how many missiles I buy, I cannot be absolutely certain that they will deter. The problem by definition, is that strategy (and war) is a dialectic of two independent, albeit other-regarding as well as self-regarding, wills.

3. With respect to deterrence, it is difficult to learn lessons from strategic history that should be useful for tomorrow. History appears to show that conventional deterrence – a concept with which I am not comfortable – fails, or fails to apply, frequently. History appears to show also that nuclear deterrence never fails. Probably I do not need to belabour the fragilities of what I have just said. Success in deterrence means inimical acts *not* committed. So, where is your evidence for that success? Sir Michael Howard tells us that 'what is beyond doubt ... is that we effectively deterred

the Soviet Union from using military force to achieve its political objectives'. How does he know that? We know for certain that our strategic behaviour in the Cold War was compatible with a non-war outcome to that contest. Yet, the non-war outcome of the Cold War may have been achieved as much despite, as because, of our defense planning. What Michael Howard wrote was reasonable and not implausible, the trouble is that he exceeded the evidence. Moreover, it could be dangerous for our security were we to take great satisfaction from his further claim that 'we have become rather expert at deterrence'. Perhaps – but, perhaps not.

4. When we move consideration of deterrence from the neat linearity of Jominian-style rational defense analysis, and instead examine a real historical case or two, the story begins to suffer from too much plot (not a common problem in Hollywood). A minor problem worth mentioning is that while you can conduct case studies of historical instances of deterrence failure, it is vastly more difficult to study cases of the success of deterrence. A closely related problem is the scholar's difficulty in studying the causes of the wars that did not happen. In other words, what caused the absence of war (which may be called peace)? At this juncture I must deploy a favourite quotation. The science fiction writer Paul Anderson once wrote: 'I have yet to see any problem, however complicated, which, when you looked at it the right way, did not become more complicated still.'

5. The challenge of deterrence is revealed as the challenge of strategy. Neither deterrence nor strategy – to which deterrence is a highly dependent variable – is comfortably, let alone reliably, reducible to a single dominant aspect. None of the great conflations, or reductive simplicities, do anything other than confuse the issue. We all have our favourite axioms. For example, 'the longer purse wins wars', 'an army marches on its stomach', 'warfare is the way of deception', 'know yourself and know the enemy', 'when in doubt double the yield', and so on and so forth. Truths about strategy are not hard to find. The problem is that strategy is a whole subject needing understanding by many truths, not just one. Thus it transpires that success in deterrence cannot be reduced to buying more, or better, military forces, to superior intelligence, to genius in command, to competence in logistics, or indeed reliably to a high score on any one (or several) of strategy's dimensions.

6. To attempt to deter is to engage in strategic behaviour, which is to say to behave within the universe of strategy. Whatever can go right, or go wrong, for strategy writ large, can go right or wrong for would-be exercises in deterrence. We cannot find short cuts to deterrence success which enable us to avoid the whole domain of strategy. Some military problems do not lend themselves to linear treatment according to a science of 'the mechanism of war', as Field Marshal Lord Wavell called it. But matters of

strategic effectiveness, matters answered at the level of their net positive or negative contribution to the course of strategic history, necessarily engage every dimension of strategy.

7. Strategy has distinguishable, but interdependent, dimensions (or factors) – much as strategy and tactics are wholly complementary. You cannot have strategy unless someone *does it* tactically; while tactical behaviour has to have strategic effect. Clausewitz identified five 'elements of strategy', and Sir Michael Howard discussed four 'dimensions of strategy'. I prefer a more granulated analysis, and besides I am a social scientist trained to ignore the principle of Occam's razor (that one should always opt for the simplest explanation compatible with the evidence), so I find that strategy has 17 dimensions. Of course, strategy does not have 17, or 5, or 4, dimensions. What we are doing is trying to capture the nature and structure of strategy, so that we can build a superior understanding from which we might derive better policy. Strategy is a practical subject. When you study strategy, the choice is yours as to how fine a mesh you want for your analytical net.

What light can be shed upon the dark places for the challenge of deterrence by a better understanding of strategy? On the one hand, my American passport tells me to be optimistic and to defy the so-called Scholar's Fallacy. The Fallacy holds that truth is achievable, and that application of that truth must lead to progress. On the other hand, my British passport tells me to be skeptical and pessimistic and to believe that the quality of strategic behaviour does not improve as we achieve better understanding, at least it does not improve for long (and perhaps not by us). Strategic understanding, in common with strategy's nature and structure, effectively has been constant throughout history. Setting these grim thoughts aside for the moment, what can we say about the challenge of deterrence deriving from a much more general treatment of the challenge of strategy?

Strategy is Difficult, Therefore Deterrence is Difficult

There may well be a sense in which I am overexplaining the blindingly obvious point that strategy, and hence deterrence, is difficult to do. My analysis is not an assault upon deterrence theory, let alone upon the value in deterrence. By all means let us deter whatever is deterrable (if only we know how to do that). There is much in common between deterrence as a strategic problem and the perils of surprise. We can and should invest heavily, if sensibly, in an intelligence system which lowers the prospects of our being surprised. However, since we know that we will be surprised, pleasantly and otherwise, our policy goal is not so much to avoid surprise as it is to avoid our suffering serious loss to the unwelcome *effect* of surprise.

Similarly, we can and should invest prudently in the nominal ability to deter across a wide spectrum of possible unfriendly acts. However, as with investment against surprise, we should expect occasional failures in our efforts to deter. The sensible policy goal, therefore, is not an unattainable zero-defect deterrence performance, but rather a deterrence performance that will fail only with consequences tolerable to us. For reasons explained already, we know that deterrence is, and inherently *has to be*, unreliable.

The achievable task, therefore, is to plan against the very occasional failures of deterrence, or its failure to apply, in such a way as both to limit the damage in the undesired context, and perhaps to add some further weight on the scales against deterrence failure. By way of a happy irony, it could be that the military program we undertake to limit damage should deterrence fail, performs on an agreeable feedback loop actually to strengthen deterrence. Ballistic Missile Defense (BMD) is a strong candidate to illustrate this speculative strategic logic.

Why is Strategy Difficult and What Does That Imply for Performance in Deterrence?

1. Strategy is the bridge between the realms of policy and military power. It is neither policy nor is it military power. Strategic effect is the consequence of military (*inter alia*) threat or action upon history. Much as the contemporary alleged information-led revolution in military affairs (RMA) is rather elusive because it is not major-platform-specific, so deterrence, and strategy even more, is apt to prove unduly ethereal for practical people. We cannot buy deterrence directly, so we spend $270 billion a year on military instruments and their supporting services, and we are fairly confident that we thereby generate a lot of 'general deterrence' and even some 'immediate deterrence'. Quite how general deterrence works we are not very sure, 'it is a mystery', as the theatrical entrepreneur in the movie *Shakespeare in Love* said of a play working well 'on the night'.

Lest I appear too hard on deterrence, I could argue, by analogy, that love and happiness similarly are conditions of mind that cannot be purchased directly and reliably. However, if you are familiar with the superior sitcom, *Frasier*, you will understand that the keys to a new Mercedes have been known to effect a mood change in a spouse. Deterrence, like its master, strategy, lacks physical reality. Documentary films about strategy are notoriously difficult to do, because of the problem of visualization. Everything that you show on film is the tactical doing of strategy, but not the elusive strategy itself. If you try to make a documentary on deterrence, what do you film? Deterrence working is, by definition, at least in most vital senses, nothing much happening. Of course, tactical behaviour intended to deter is being 'done' and can be filmed. But how do you show minds deterred and decisions for inaction?

2. A fundamental difficulty for deterrence is the sheer complexity in the structure and functioning of strategy. As I have observed already, strategy has many dimensions, all of which always are on the strategic field of play at all times, even though each will play with a significance distinctive to each unique conflict. The writings on deterrence by social scientists and historians, which point plausibly to particular reasons why deterrence either failed, or might have failed, can be strengthened if we place a general template for strategy over their detailed arguments. To explain, because deterrence is a strategic intention and, if successful, a strategic condition, it has to be subject to what the Baron Antoine Henri de Jomini and others have understood to be the eternal lore of strategy.

Appreciation of the complexity of strategy, its non-trivially chaotic (partial) non-linearity, should alert us to what can go wrong for deterrence. If strategy is 'made' of such elements as: people; society; culture; politics; ethics; economics and logistics; organization; military administration; information and intelligence; strategic theory and doctrine; technology; military operations; command; geography; friction; the adversary; and time – it is not hard to understand that there are many, many ways in which strategic performance, including performance in deterrence, can be impaired. Some substitution across dimensions certainly is possible. To deter successfully one need not attain a perfect score in relative excellence on each of these 17 dimensions. However, it is possible that a truly awful shortfall on any one, let alone several, could fatally abort efforts to deter.

3. If it is hard to train strategists, it has to be exceptionally hard to train strategists to perform well for deterrence. The leading reason why it is hard to train strategists is, of course, because there is no career path in strategy. Military professionals, with scarcely any exceptions, 'do' tactics and operations, not strategy. Strategy is well above their pay grade. To be unquestionably superior in the ability to command soldiers in battle, does not, *ipso facto*, yield you insight into strategy. Strategy, please recall, is about the *use* of engagements, not about the engagements themselves, no matter how well they are conducted. A US President will be awesomely competent in domestic politics, but even if he or she has forgotten more about foreign policy than George W. Bush will ever know, that knowledge itself yields no skill in strategy. The strategist has to build and hold the bridge between politics and military power. The would-be deterree must cope with a structural difficulty that is extreme even by the exacting standards of strategy. Specifically, the would-be deterrer has to calculate, which is to say *guess*, how much, of what kind, of military power as threat or in use is likely to have the desired effect on culturally alien minds. As my

colleague Keith Payne reminds me in his writings, history is replete with cases of intended deterrence when the intending-deterrer was woefully ignorant of the state of the minds that were the targets. Now, strategy is difficult enough when all you have to do is devise ways in which an enemy can be controlled physically. How much more difficult is the mission of deterrence, when you need to guess how an imperfectly understood enemy (i.e., real individuals in real policy processes) will choose to respond to threats (which threats?).

4. As a further perspective upon the complexity of strategy described already, there is the necessary and inescapable fact that for the strategist, when compared with the tactician and the operational artist, there is the maximum possible number of sources of error. As Keith Payne will tell you, the reasons for possible deterrence failures are as extensive as is the domain of strategy itself. The problem could be one or several of the following: a policy that asks the impossible of the enemy; a policy that the enemy genuinely does not comprehend; a policy that is not communicated clearly enough; threats that enemy political leaders find hugely deterring, but, alas, they do not enjoy reliable command of their country's armed forces; deterring threats in words, but a military instrument for deterrence manifestly, or falsely believed by the enemy to be so, incapable of performing as advertised ... and so on.

5. Finally, as an all too significantly worthy special element of strategy that can frustrate policy intentions, we need to flag the importance of the adversary. It is tempting for strategic thinkers and defense planners to slight the probably unique reality of the living, breathing, historically unique enemy. We tend to be more comfortable with the world that we control, or appear to control. So, as noted earlier, we refer to *the* deterrent, an assertion of unilateral merit over what is surely a relational variable. Only the enemy can decide whether or not our armed forces are *the* deterrent. Those forces are graded for their deterrent performance abroad, not by us at home. The apparent fact *to us* that our forces should deter, is really neither here nor there. Because the enemy, as well as playing a legitimizing role, is also an inconvenient wild card which threatens the otherwise orderly world of our strategic thought and defense planning, in practice it is always tempting not to take him seriously.

I do not mean to imply intentional dishonesty – at least I do not think that I do. My point rather is that since, as a general rule, we cannot know, *really know*, what an enemy will do, we are obliged to make some prudent, and hopefully well-educated, guesses. It is not difficult to forget that we have invented an American-style adversary, whose thought processes, we assume, are accessible to, and therefore predictable by, us. We appreciate that rationality and reason are different, but it is exceedingly difficult to pursue, let alone operationalize, that recognition.

The point is that a culturally alien foe is likely to behave quite *rationally* in his own strategic terms of sensible ends and prudent means, but that behaviour may not be *reasonable* to us. If we intend to overwhelm an enemy physically, we may assume as a practical matter that sheer brute force on our part will compensate tolerably well for those areas of our ignorance about him. But, in contrast, if we seek to deter, we are voting for a strategic context wherein everything locally individual about the enemy – which we may comprehend only poorly – will play at a premium. After all, with the deterrence mission we seek to influence how and what an enemy thinks.

Fate and Self-Help

It is important to recognize the essential unreliability of deterrence, a recognition rendered more solid, perhaps, when it is anchored upon understanding of the permanent nature of strategy. It is also important, however, not to overstate the unreliability of deterrence, and not to exaggerate the chaotic non-linearity of strategic phenomena. Deterrence can, and does, work. Strategic effect can be predicted quite well from an accurate assessment of its dimensions in their dynamic functioning. But, because deterrence is residually unreliable, and because strategic outcomes are not entirely predictable, it is prudent for us to give fate a helping hand. We have to provide against deterrence failure, just as we have to provide for unexpected twists and turns in the course of strategic history. The challenge is for us to avoid capture by our own desire for convenient certainties. To try to deter, in common with efforts to win in war, are rolls of the 'iron dice'. Deep down, we know this. But, it can be impolitic to admit to uncertainty, even structural uncertainly, and the pretense of strategic knowledge can be habit-forming. We become victims of our own convenient oversimplifications.

Part Two

Rethinking Problems and Responses

Ten Reasons Why Nuclear Deterrence Could Fail: The Case for Reassessing US Nuclear Policies and Plans

JOHN M. WEINSTEIN

While the Cold War is over, serious developments threaten US national security. In recent years, we have seen chemical agent attacks; increasingly sophisticated information warfare threats that could cripple our financial, transportation, communications, and power infrastructures; and growing collaboration between rogue states, terrorists, and non-state actors whose pernicious aims are matched by substantial and growing capabilities. More worrisome are the threats of biological weapons, along with the continuing proliferation of advanced long-range missiles and other military technologies.

Perhaps the most disconcerting development is the continuing spread of nuclear weapons and weapon technology. In the future, the United States will encounter state and, perhaps, non-state adversaries armed with nuclear weapons. Most certainly, these weapons will continue to proliferate, our counter-proliferation initiatives notwithstanding, because their military effectiveness and political impact make them extraordinarily attractive. They may be used to defend a state's legitimate interests against an adversary that possesses overwhelming conventional forces; they may confer international political stature on otherwise poor countries; they inflate the egos of megalomaniacal leaders; and they bolster national pride, deflecting domestic attention from national concerns and problems.

Nuclear weapons can neither deter nor provide an appropriate response to all threats. It is difficult to imagine how the threat of nuclear retaliation would deter a terrorist or other non-state actor from smuggling a nuclear or biological weapon into the US. Similarly, a nuclear response to a cyber terrorist attack against our financial and banking systems would be difficult to justify. Still, these awesome weapons retain a critical role in the defense of our most critical security interests. Besides deterring Russian and

The views expressed here are those of the author and do not necessarily reflect the official policy or position of the US Nuclear Command and Control System Support Staff or the US government.

Chinese 'adventures' backed up by their strategic nuclear arsenals, there are other palpable threats nuclear weapons can deter. The disturbing reality is, however, that nuclear deterrence could easily fail in the future due to any of the following political, cultural, technological, and bureaucratic reasons.

False Sense of Nuclear Security

After 50 years of the Cold War, many believe the demise of the Soviet Union makes the threat of nuclear war obsolete and the need for such weapons irrelevant. Such thinking suggests, to quote Winston Churchill's definition of second marriages, the triumph of hope over experience. Russia is beset with numerous social, political, and economic problems that could result in unpredictable and uncontrollable developments. These problems include: an economy in disarray; widespread corruption and incompetence within the bureaucracy, resulting in widespread popular unrest and the devolution of power from national level to regional governmental and private (both legal and illegal) entities; growing centrifugal forces of ethnic and national separatism; and the continuing vitality of extremist leaders who view relations with the United States as a 'zero-sum' game. Within this context, Russia has maintained a large and lethal nuclear arsenal and, like the Chinese, continues to modernize these forces. Moreover, Russia's new military doctrine recognizes its declining conventional capabilities and now relies more heavily on earlier, and even first use of nuclear forces.

Finally, Russia's ballistic missile attack-warning system is deteriorating. In 1995, for instance, the Russians generated their nuclear forces in response to the launch of a weather satellite because their deteriorating ballistic missile attack warning system failed to discern the non-threatening nature of the launch. Whether due to an error, or an unanticipated radical shift in US-Russian relations such as occurred in the first part of this decade, the threat of nuclear war remains a valid concern.

The deadly mix of proliferating nuclear weapons and missile technologies, discontent within the Russian military that could weaken nuclear weapons command and control, and terrorism, overlaid on smoldering ethnic, nationalist, and religious conflicts keep the nuclear threat alive against the US homeland, our forces, and our allies. Can we assume that because our arsenal of nuclear weapons helped to deter war with the Soviet Union, it will continue to do so against new adversaries, both state and non-state, with different social, political, and economic agenda, values, capabilities, and cost/benefit calculations?

Failure to Recognize the New Dimensions of the Deterrence Problem.

Deterring the Soviet Union was a relatively manageable proposition. Each superpower understood the other's interests and capabilities. Additionally, years of arms control agreements and other venues of face-to-face, high-level negotiations fostered mutual understanding, if not always accord. And when potential disputes threatened US-USSR relations, conflict resolution mechanisms, such as the Hot Line, helped ensure crisis stability. Unfortunately, such understandings and mechanisms do not exist between the US and many current and potential adversaries.

The fact is that the deterrent calculus has become more complex, and new complicated issues are arising. At a minimum, on-going discussions on deterrence must address:

- What is the relationship between deterrence and other concepts, such as compellance, dissuasion, defense, and denial and how do we integrate these concepts into strategy, doctrine, and operations with respect to new and emerging adversaries?

- How will the growing consolidation and internationalization of the telecommunications industry affect the Integrated Warning/Attack Assessment system? Will foreign ownership of parts of the Public Switch Network reduce the security of critical nuclear command and control communications?

- How can we ensure required survivability and endurance of nuclear weapons operating equipment while we increase our reliance on Commercial Off-the-Shelf (COTS) products? How do we ensure the continued security and reliability of foreign-produced hardware, software, and firmware? How will we continue to certify equipment for nuclear use?

- As the US develops national and/or theater defenses, how will US Nuclear Command and Control System communications, and facilities be affected? What will be the impacts on nuclear command and control emergency action procedures, priorities, protocols, and programs? Will we be able to maintain a 'man in the loop' for critical decisions as timelines shorten?

- How do we deter adversaries who are financially/economically linked to US through the internationalization of businesses or who control resources critical to our own economy or those of our allies?

- How do we deter assaults on US territory or infrastructure (e.g., cyber attacks, biological attacks carried out clandestinely by non-state actors or actors whose affiliation we cannot identify)?

- Through which mechanisms will we pursue conflict resolution and escalation control with non-state actors, such as the Russian mafia or drug cartels, which may acquire a nuclear or some other horrific weapon? Whom do we target and how and with whom do we negotiate?

- Finally, a successful deterrent strategy must recognize that deterrence may fail. Our debate on deterrence requirements and future courses of action must address how to deter follow-on use of these weapons (i.e., escalation control/intra-war deterrence), defenses, vulnerabilities to existing and emerging threats, and consequence management.

Belief in Antiseptic Warfare

War is a bloody and brutish endeavor. Our belief in the efficacy of technology, bolstered by 1991 Gulf War footage of smart bombs unerringly destroying their targets, has fostered two dangerous and faulty perceptions.

The first is that wars can be fought without the significant loss of American lives. Clearly, an adversary armed even with primitive nuclear, biological, or chemical weapons or with conventional forces armed with long-range missiles or other sophisticated military technology on the market can exact a terrible price against US forces.

The second misperception is that high-tech conventional weapons can make nuclear weapons superfluous. Apart from their role in deterring nuclear attacks against the US homeland, our forces, or our allies, there are certain targets, such as shallow buried bunkers with biological agents, against which only a nuclear weapon is effective. Moreover, there are other targets that advanced conventional munitions cannot destroy (e.g., the increasing numbers of deep underground command posts and special weapons storage sites). Furthermore, the effectiveness of laser-guided wonder weapons can be thwarted by bad weather, smoke and other counter-measures, and the reliance on stand-off weapons may not suffice to shape an adversary's perceptions of our political resolve and calculations of consequences along lines consistent with US national interests.

Self-Deterrence

The foregoing is likely to result in self-deterrence, the belief we can never and should never use nuclear weapons under any circumstances. Unrealistic expectations about the antiseptic nature of warfare, unwillingness to put Americans in harm's way, or an adversary's view that the US will not vigorously defend its legitimate supreme interests could undermine deterrence. An adversary's perception that the US is unwilling to risk casualties or to employ decisive firepower in defense of our interests may result in miscalculations of our intent and resolve. The widespread belief of many Americans that nuclear weapons will never be used because they are irrelevant or too horrible deters only us. If an adversary believes that certain options, including nuclear options, are not available to the President, erroneous assumptions of likely US retaliation, conflict escalation, and/or failure to terminate conflict at the lowest level of violence become more likely.

Fractionalization of National Security

The components of national security are not discrete and unrelated entities. Nuclear weapons cannot be viewed apart from conventional forces and intercontinental-range nuclear weapons should not be viewed differently from shorter-range nuclear forces, which are also strategic in effect. There must be planning to integrate nuclear forces with ballistic missile defenses as the latter are developed. Deterrence cannot be viewed separately from the possibility of its failure and, hence, the need for consequence and disaster management. Finally, military capabilities must be integrated with economic, diplomatic, technological, commerce, and other elements of state power. If these elements are held hostage to proprietary, bureaucratic strictures rather than integrated into a seamless web in support of national security objectives, we fail to exploit available synergy. We may also come to expect conventional military power to substitute for statecraft and other non-lethal mechanisms to pursue our interests. In short, we may become too dependent on military operations because we do not appreciate their limitations. The resulting diminution of deterrence in an age of nuclear proliferation is an increasingly dangerous trend.

Lack of Attention by Senior Leaders to Nuclear Matters

A recent Defense Science Board Task Force concluded that senior government leaders do not pay regular attention to nuclear weapons matters. Another high-level study, conducted in 1998 at the National Defense University, arrived at the same conclusion. Whether due to complacency, competing priorities, or self-deterrence, the resulting lack of focused and integrated management has significant negative effects: adequate funding for required programs is not forthcoming, serious problems remain uncorrected, and the morale of dedicated people trying to do more with less has begun to slip. As a result of the lack of regular high-level attention to nuclear matters beyond arms control, non- and counterproliferation, and confidence building measures, the frequency of realistic exercises with senior participation declines, aging facilities and equipment are not replaced, and capabilities required for nuclear weapons safety, security, control, and reliability decline.

This slide is worsened by the recognition throughout the military, the Office of the Secretary of Defense, and the national nuclear laboratories, that the nuclear weapons career fields have few opportunities for promotion to senior leadership positions. Consequently, it becomes more difficult to recruit the smartest and most highly motivated candidates into the nuclear community.

Likewise, retaining an experienced cadre of competence in core areas becomes problematic. Nuclear weapons operations, to include those that assure against the unauthorized or inadvertent use of nuclear weapons, must remain a zero-defect enterprise. The loss of personnel with unique expertise in key operational and support areas further reduces nuclear surety.

These trends foster self-deterrence by leaders who do not understand these weapons or who doubt their efficacy and/or effectiveness. These trends also cause uncertainty among our allies whose security is tied to the deterrent umbrella provided by our nuclear weapons. The only certainty, erroneous or not, may exist in the perceptions of adversaries who doubt the US is willing or able to fulfill its nuclear declaratory policy.

Reduced Survivability of Nuclear Weapons and Assets that Provide Critical Supporting Capabilities

One result of reduced spending in the nuclear area is declining budgets for programs to harden key satellite, communications, and other critical nuclear and non-nuclear supporting equipment and facilities to the effects of nuclear-induced electromagnetic pulse (EMP). Another result is the failure to spend funds to maintain the hardness against EMP, radio-frequency weapons, and natural phenomena designed into certain military systems.

These potential vulnerabilities may be compounded by our increasing reliance on commercial off-the-shelf (COTS) technology, whose components lack the radiological hardness, ruggedness, quality control, and life-cycle certifiability required for many nuclear systems. Also, since COTS hardware and software are often produced overseas, we cannot be certain components do not contain trap doors, viruses, logic bombs, and other characteristics that could cause our systems to fail or operate in an undesirable manner. If nuclear weapons and supporting systems, such as the systems that warn of a missile attack, do not survive or do not operate as planned, they will not support robust and flexible deterrence.

Strategy-Yield Mismatch

Nuclear weapons *can* deter a wide range of nuclear and non-nuclear threats *if* they possess flexible characteristics and capabilities *and* are matched to realistic political and military objectives. This flexibility requires a range of yields, ability to penetrate the earth, various heights of burst and fusing options, etc. such that their retaliatory use is perceived as proportional to the attack. However, many of the weapons in our current arsenal may be inappropriate (e.g., yield is too large, unable to penetrate, inappropriate fusing options, escalatory) for deterring the evolving broad range of threats to our interests. The majority of our nuclear arsenal, and all the weapons on day-to-day alert, are large-yield weapons on ballistic missiles. Is a 100–500 kiloton warhead, which may have to overfly Russia or China in a crisis, appropriate for deterring a rogue state with a few nuclear, biological, or chemical weapons or for responding to such an attack?

Much of our existing arsenal was designed to destroy Soviet missile silos, underground command centers, and other hardened military targets. While it is appropriate to protect these capable weapons in arms control negotiations, we need to ask if we have the right numbers of weapons with the right mix of operational characteristics, delivery platforms, and necessary infrastructure support to deter lesser, and perhaps, more likely nuclear threats. If not, we should explore which modifications to existing weapons (preferably within the framework of the Comprehensive Test Ban Treaty) could be developed by the national nuclear laboratories.

We must also reevaluate theater nuclear doctrine and capabilities. These lower yield weapons may offer the greatest contributions to deterrence because they possess many of the characteristics that would make the threat of their use credible to a rogue state armed with nuclear, chemical, or biological weapons.

Finally, we must exercise our strategy regularly and ensure the participation of senior military and civilian leaders in these exercises so they may become familiar with their complex nuclear weapons-related responsibilities. Capable weapons lacking well-conceived doctrine and effective plans have limited military utility and provide little support to deterrence.

Loss of Operational Capability Reduces the President's Flexibility

At the beginning of the 1990s, potential adversaries contemplating the use of nuclear, chemical, or biological weapons against the US homeland, our forces, or our adversaries knew the President possessed a potent arsenal of broad capabilities that could be brought to bear in a timely manner. Moreover, these forces were exercised regularly so it was widely perceived that they could be used effectively if so directed by the President. Saddam Hussein's knowledge of our capability and his perception of our intent likely contributed to his decision not to employ his biological and chemical weapons.

In the last ten years, however, US nuclear forces have undergone significant changes reducing their number and the timeliness with which they can be brought to bear in a crisis or to deter or respond to an adversary's attack. For instance, the Navy no longer carries nuclear weapons on surface ships, no longer can deliver nuclear weapons from carriers or shore airbases, and submarines cannot immediately fire nuclear Tomahawk cruise missiles (all of which are stored in the continental US) without a lengthy period (weeks) of regeneration and transit to execution areas; nuclear howitzer and missile artillery have been withdrawn from Europe and Korea; strategic bombers are no longer maintained on continuous strip alert; and readiness requirements of other forces are being relaxed.

Additionally, operational characteristics associated with inter-continental ballistic missiles (ICBMs) and sea-launched ballistic missiles (SLBMs) (e.g. each missile carries multiple, high-yield warheads; a trajectory that passes over Russian territory; and the possibility that the intentions behind the launch of a limited number of missiles could be misconstrued by another nuclear power) could make their use risky and undesirable in a crisis with a rogue state.

In short, the President has fewer ready nuclear weapons with the proper mix of operational characteristics whose use or threat of use can support US deterrence, escalation control, and prompt conflict termination objectives in a world characterized by an increasing number of rogue states with nuclear, chemical, and/or biological weapons.

Fuzzy Jargon Begets Fuzzy Thinking

The term *du jour* in discussions on deterrence and national policy is 'weapons of mass destruction', or WMD. This term lumps nuclear, biological, and chemical weapons into a general category whose title alludes to their horrific effects. Such an omnibus category suggests that nuclear weapons could be used to respond to attacks using chemical or biological weapons, thereby improving deterrence by bolstering the credibility of their retaliatory use against such horrific weapons. However, the use of this term in internal Department of Defence and government strategy and doctrine deliberations may actually undermine meaningful discussions about deterrence by insinuating that nuclear, chemical, and biological weapons are interchangeable.

These weapons differ immensely with respect to lethality, logistics requirements, employment concepts, time to effect, area coverage, history of use, moral/ethical/legal considerations, the abilities to identify the attacker and predict effects, and many more important factors. Placing nuclear weapons in the same category as the other two prevents the development of clear deterrence concepts and strategies that effectively employ their respective characteristics. To treat all weapons the same is like preparing to make an ocean voyage without regard to the type of ship.

Deterrence has become more complex. We need precise terminology to evaluate options and develop effective plans. The sooner we exorcise the WMD shorthand from our deterrence vocabulary, the sooner we will be able to develop credible, flexible nuclear policies and plans serving deterrence and our national interests.

Conclusion

The future security environment will be characterized by more diverse threats, from unpredictable directions, and by more diverse state and non-state actors. While nuclear weapons cannot deter all threats or respond appropriately to all instances in which deterrence fails, they do have a unique and irreplaceable role in deterring a broad range of hostile acts against the US, our forces, and our allies. Further, effective US nuclear forces support the goal of reducing the proliferation of nuclear weapons among states that may feel the need to develop their own nuclear deterrent if they perceive the US nuclear umbrella lacks credibility. It is time to reassess our nuclear policies and plans and to take such steps as to ensure that deterrence remains credible and flexible in an increasingly uncertain, emboldened, and dangerous world.

Some Possible Surprises in Our Nuclear Future

GEORGE H. QUESTER

A great number of people around the world are predicting, and hoping for, a dramatic reduction in the nuclear arsenals of Russia and the United States,[1] regarding this as only natural after the end of the Cold War, and expecting this to eliminate a great menace to human life. Some of such people favor policies of 'finite deterrence' or 'minimum deterrence', where the superpower nuclear arsenals might go down to 100 or 200 warheads, instead of the tens of thousands that were accumulated in the years of Cold War rivalry. Others would advocate a total elimination of such weapons, consistent with various pledges issued over the years in Washington and Moscow, consistent with the terms of Article VI of the Nuclear Non-Proliferation Treaty (NPT), with any 'finite' force level of 100 or 200 being only the necessary interval phase on the way to the ultimate goal: zero.

The political and symbolic advantages of getting rid of nuclear weapons may seem obvious given the widespread endorsement such reductions draw, and some high-level former civilian defense officials and former military commanders have endorsed a move toward zero. Reducing the total of nuclear weapons would certainly seem to reduce the risk of an accident where such nuclear weapons, perhaps because of insanity or other form of insubordination, came into use,[2] and it would reduce the implicit political poison and insult that derives from societies threatening each other with 'mutual assured destruction'.

The contrary argument here will be, however, that a world of much lower nuclear force levels is basically a very unknown situation for all of us, a situation which may spring some unpleasant surprises. And, even if it might seem that a totally nuclear-weapons-free world would be desirable, there are risks that the *approach* to such a world might be very dangerous.

The last time the world experienced a situation totally free of nuclear weapons, it was immersed in the bloody battles of World War II; battles dramatically brought to an end by the sudden devastation of Hiroshima and Nagasaki. The last time the world experienced a confrontation of very small and 'finite' nuclear forces, it was experiencing the tensions of 'bomber gaps' and 'missile gaps', as Albert Wohlstetter and his colleagues at the RAND Corporation projected a 'delicate balance of terror'.[3]

What will follow is a discussion of some possible surprises in our nuclear future, if (because of continuing negotiations between the US and the Russian Federation, and/or because of budgetary constrictions on the military forces of these two countries) the reduction of nuclear arsenals proceeds apace. Since the new situation is so fraught with the unknown, not all the surprises have to be unpleasant and disappointing here, and some upbeat possibilities will also be noted. But, since so many people see nuclear arms reductions as a predominantly positive accomplishment, the first task will be to examine some of the more frightening and negative possibilities of surprise.

Strategic Instability

One of our most urgent tasks in the nuclear field, most would agree, is to avoid the kind of strategic situation where each side fears that the other is tempted to strike first, and where each sees advantages to preempting or heading off such an opposing first strike.[4] This was the situation of the Cold War confrontation before missiles were introduced and perfected, as Strategic Air Command (SAC) bombers and their Soviet equivalent might have been able to win a World War III by striking first at the airbases of the opposing side.

What has made such a 'splendid first strike' basically unthinkable for the years since 1960 has been the tremendous expansion of 'overkill' in the nuclear arsenals of the two sides, reinsured by the basing of thermonuclear retaliatory second-strike forces onboard submarines and in hardened land-based underground silos; it thus became basically unimaginable that either superpower could ever launch a first-strike that would protect its own cities from retaliation.

With enormously redundant retaliatory nuclear forces, there was thus no need for haste or nervousness in launching retaliatory strikes. 'Strategic stability' or 'crisis stability' requires that each side feel safe waiting in ambiguous situations.[5] The introduction of submarine-basing and large force levels made the nuclear confrontation considerably more stable and relaxed, as compared with the smaller warhead totals and aircraft delivery systems which had been the total of the nuclear forces so much alarming Wohlstetter and his colleagues in the 1950s.

The Russian and American negotiators of Strategic Arms Reduction Treaty (START) reductions have indeed clearly shown an awareness of the importance of strategic stability, of avoiding setting the stage for a preemptive 'war nobody wanted', as multiple independent re-entry vehicle (MIRVed) missiles were placed at the top of the list of systems to be phased out.

Yet as the Russian and American force totals are reduced, and as the momentum of popular feelings or budgetary pressures continues, the risk remains that crisis stability may suffer. One sees this even at the present moment, amid lingering reports that the Russian nuclear arsenal is being kept worrisomely close to a policy of launch-on-warning.[6] The dubious seaworthiness of the Russian strategic-missile submarines, and the general reduction in Russian nuclear force totals, have thus apparently caused Moscow's civilian and military leadership to feel insecure, insecure in a way that threatens the safety of the cities of the United States.

If one tried to move all the way to zero, or simply tried to reduce the major nuclear arsenals to several hundred warheads, one might then see much more of this kind of insecurity. This would be a world where a 'clever briefer' on one side might offer his civilian superior a supposed opportunity to launch a successful first-strike, or where a similar briefer could persuade his chief that the opposing side was contemplating such a strike.

Preemptive situations bring out the worst in all the societies, even where the political disagreements between them have become minimal, and some would indeed see the outbreak of World War I as an illustration of such preemptive motivations.[7] Much the worst fear that one could imagine here would come with an American briefing by which the Russian command was seen as incorrectly anticipating an American nuclear Pearl Harbor sneak attack, and as planning to preempt such an attack – for which the only possible American response would then be to preempt the preemption.

Such a cycle of self-confirming hypotheses was what many expected might cause World War III in the 1950s, just as it may be what caused World War I in 1914, something close to what game theory describes as prisoners' dilemma.[8] Such a cycle was seen as out of the question in the enormous nuclear arsenals of 'overkill' that had been accumulated by the 1980s. But, the disappointing point would be, this is the kind of nerve-wracking scenario that may spring to life again, if and when we try to move to zero, or even if we try to get to much lower numbers closer to zero. To repeat, we may even now be seeing some of this worrisome interaction coming back as the direct result of the collapse of the Soviet Union.

Nuclear Proliferation

We have thus far not mentioned the other nuclear forces in the world, outside the United States and Russia. Many Americans might assume that the best way for Washington and Moscow to discourage the proliferation of nuclear weapons to additional countries is to set the good example of substantial, or total, nuclear disarmament, as indeed was written into the Non-Proliferation Treaty (NPT) when that treaty was established as a buffer against nuclear weapons spread.

One of the arguments directed against the original drafts of the NPT, and even against the final draft, was that it was fundamentally uneven and unfair, allowing five countries, the United States and the Soviet Union, and Britain, France and China, to possess nuclear weapons, and forbidding any other signatory to the treaty from possessing them.[9] To relieve this sense of unfairness, the nuclear-weapons states thus supposedly agreed to the insertion of Article VI of the treaty, and it would then presumably be important for them to comply with its terms, calling for 'nuclear disarmament, and ... general and complete disarmament under strict and effective international control'.[10]

At the various review conferences incorporated into the workings of the treaty, and on other occasions, it was always possible for Washington and Moscow to cite the reductions undertaken to date in their nuclear arsenals; but critics could then counter that these reductions had not gone far enough, and would have to be accelerated, with nothing being fair or acceptable until the American and former Soviet nuclear weapons totals had been reduced all the way to zero.

As an example of how superpower nuclear force reductions can indeed have a desirable influence, especially where the countries involved have shifted to democracy, one might look at Brazil and Argentina, which were both suspected of moving toward nuclear weapons programs of their own in the 1960s and 1970s, but which have now renounced such weapons by signing first the Latin American Nuclear Free Zone treaty, and then the NPT, and by submitting first to a sort of mutual inspection of their nuclear research facilities, and then to the safeguards of the International Atomic Energy Agency (IAEA).[11]

Yet it is entirely possible that the power of example will not always be so effective here, even where governments are democratic. India and Pakistan have moved across the line to an open and explicit possession of nuclear weapons, despite the reductions in the numbers of such weapons controlled by Washington and Moscow.[12]

And there are indeed several lines of logical reasoning why superpower disarmament might encounter yet another unpleasant surprise here, making nuclear proliferation more likely rather than less.

First of all, there have, over the decades since Hiroshima, been several countries around the world where scientists or military commanders or political leaders would have liked to promote a national nuclear weapons program, for the simple enhancement of national power or glory, or personal power and glory that would come with this. One can fairly easily find examples of such leaders in Sweden and Argentina, and Brazil and Australia, and in Japan, etc.

What stopped such programs from going any further was often the counter-argument that any 'nth' nuclear weapons program here would be totally outclassed by the enormous size of the existing superpower nuclear arsenals. To get into the major leagues of being a nuclear-weapons state would entail very substantial expenditures and effort, and not merely the harnessing of plutonium spin-offs from nuclear power reactors.

As we look forward to a hypothetical world of a much smaller American and Russian nuclear arsenal, however, any similar advocates of nuclear proliferation would have a somewhat easier case to make, in terms of very selfish national interest, as it will take a much smaller number of warheads, and a smaller economic sacrifice, to break into the major leagues.

A different kind of argument was related to countries that needed the protection of the American nuclear umbrella of 'extended nuclear deterrence', West Germany and South Korea being the two prime examples, but not the only conceivable cases.[13] These were countries facing the risk of an invasion by the overwhelming conventional forces of a hostile neighbor, and seeking a nuclear deterrent to prevent such an invasion from being launched.

If the United States had extensive nuclear forces, and was ready to deploy some of them to create a credible threat of nuclear escalation, such allies might feel that they did not need to seek nuclear forces of their own. If the United States nuclear force has been substantially or totally eliminated, however, and if Washington has decided to de-emphasize nuclear forces for reinforcing alliance commitments, then any state in such a future exposed situation might feel much more driven to seek a nuclear force of its own.[14]

What holds for a major reduction in American nuclear forces might be even more worrisome for a total nuclear disarmament. If Moscow and Washington have totally eliminated their nuclear forces, the world will be plagued by rumors that one or the other of them has been cheating, and has retained some of such weapons. In such a world, there will also be rumors about Brazil or Japan, or Iran or Germany, with some countries then tempted to cheat merely to protect themselves, and with a few countries tempted to cheat because a unique possession of nuclear weapons may indeed give their country some tremendous additional political clout.[15]

We just above discussed the risks of 'crisis instability' in a confrontation of greatly reduced nuclear forces, where each side might be burdened by scenarios and fears of someone launching a 'splendid first strike'. Parallel to this would be scenarios and fears of someone else being the first to cheat, of someone else cheating because they think that we are cheating.

In the nuclear world, it is more generally desirable to avoid the situations where fears become self-confirming, where separate countries get into cycles of preemption. Such cycles could cause wars to happen that would otherwise have been avoided. And, not quite as bad, but also very unpleasant, they could cause rounds of arms race and proliferation to emerge that would otherwise have been avoided.

One general goal of nuclear disarmers, they will often stress, is to reduce the perceived importance of such weapons, as well as reducing the numbers of them retained in the world's arsenals. Yet reducing their numbers may not always fit so well with reducing their importance. Perhaps nuclear weapons are not to be seen anymore as the currency of international power. But an elementary monetary principle is that the value of a unit of any particular currency goes up as the total of that currency in circulation is decreased.

A 'rudimentary' nuclear stockpile of several dozen atomic bombs might count for very little when Washington and Moscow have thousands. But if the superpowers have cut down into the hundreds, several dozen might be very important.

The Immorality of Mutual Assured Destruction

What has kept the peace in the nuclear age has been largely the ability of each side to retaliate against the cities of the other, no matter what the other side has done in its initial first-strike counterforce attack. The potential suffering of the innocent residents of such cities, as they are subjected to a largely immoral countervalue attack, suffices to keep any leadership from becoming guilty of launching a World War III.[16]

Students in courses on nuclear strategy and nuclear deterrence often come away from the subject by concluding that they can live with this (the harnessing of a bad means to a good end) because 'it works'. But ordinary people are more typically revulsed by the idea of 'mutual assured destruction', and do not want to have to think about it.[17]

Official discussions of the targeting doctrines for nuclear weapons thus often label all of the civilian suffering that would occur as 'inadvertent collateral damage', and the 'official' target of even a second-strike retaliatory strike would be the military forces of the enemy. Someone who sees the civilian suffering of a second-strike as a necessary part of mutual deterrence would regard such 'official' targeting doctrines as useful euphemisms, misleading and hypocritical, but understandable given the Western moral traditions that make it unacceptable to aim intentionally at civilian targets.

A certain degree of hypocrisy and obfuscation may thus be welcomed by someone who sees how such deterrence is at odds with most of Western morality (by which a bad means can not be used to serve a good end), but who also supports mutual nuclear deterrence because it may seem the only reliable way to keep such weapons from being used. The Roman Catholic Bishops' Statement on nuclear deterrence issued in 1983[18] brought to the surface some of the important issues of morality here, issues which will remain difficult to deal with whenever they are confronted directly.

Nuclear deterrence by mutual assured destruction may well be acceptable, because we have no other choice. But any parallel mechanism in another part of human life would be rejected out of hand.

Suppose that someone suggested reducing the murder rate in our cities by, when the actual murderer could not be apprehended, punishing his wife and children; such a suggestion would be rejected out of hand as a return to the Dark Ages, as an approach totally incompatible with all the progress that we have made in our civilization. But this is the mechanism by which nuclear peace has been maintained, and it may be maintainable only because we do not admit this to ourselves.

The incompatibility of mutual deterrence with traditional morality may then generate one more nasty surprise if nuclear disarmament continues. At higher force levels, it has always remained possible to pretend that extensive arrays of *military* targets are being aimed at, with the ensuing toll in civilian life being inadvertent and collateral. If the totals of nuclear warheads sink down into the hundreds, however, it will become more and more necessary that their only target be labeled as cities, that is, that the civilian life of the opposite side be openly and deliberately targeted.

The outright advocates of 'finite deterrence' sometimes are intellectually honest enough to admit that cities would have to be the target.[19] Advocates of total nuclear disarmament more typically avoid the issue by saying that nothing would be targeted once all nuclear weapons were eliminated, brushing aside the possibly very dangerous transition period when the last hundreds or dozens of nuclear weapons were still in place. As outlined above, the problem of crisis stability would be very serious at these low levels; and the one antidote to instability, and preemptive dreams and fears, has been the reminder that cities would be assuredly destroyed.

Low numbers thus are likely to make clear the morally ugly nature of nuclear deterrence, when higher numbers have made it possible to blur this ugliness. As illustrated by the excitement provoked by the Roman Catholic Bishops' Statement, we faced a risk for all the years of the Cold War that the world's publics would be revulsed by the nature of nuclear deterrence, if they had to confront it too directly. This is a risk that we still face.

Invidious Comparison

We have still said very little about nuclear forces other than those of America and Russia, except to warn, as above, that deep reductions in the superpower arsenals may encourage nuclear proliferation rather than discourage it.

When asked how the START negotiations are to affect France, Britain and China, advocates of nuclear disarmament will respond that the early rounds of START were most appropriately limited to the superpowers, the largest offenders in terms of amassing nuclear destructive power, but that later rounds will of course have to draw these second-tier powers in as well. But how are they to be drawn in?[20]

One version would be to propose similar proportions of decrease for China and France and Britain, and for India and Pakistan, and Israel, as everyone moves to zero, or everyone goes to finite deterrence levels. But each of these states would respond that they are already at finite levels, that it would be outrageous to ask one of them to reduce their arsenal by 90 per cent, merely because Moscow and Washington had slashed their enormous ranges of overkill by 90 per cent. One sometimes thus hears Chinese arms policy analysts speculating that their country should not disarm at all in the nuclear field until Moscow and Washington come down to Beijing's level, or perhaps that Beijing should even move up in the total of nuclear weapons it possesses, as part of meeting Washington and Moscow on their way down.

What is indeed very likely is that some or all of these states will demand a 'fairness' and 'equality of treatment' here, by which they would regard it as a national insult if nuclear force levels were negotiated any lower for them than for Russia or America. France or China did not demand parity and equality with the United States in the Cold War because the American and Russian force levels were so very high, so impossible to match. But if Russian and American nuclear force reductions make for a level that is not so physically unattainable, it is not clear that other states will renounce the right to match this.

Thus another unpleasant surprise may be that China insists on negotiating force levels identical to those of the United States and the Russian Federation, and also that France and Britain insist on this equality for themselves, and that the US Congress will have to decide what to do about this.

One can easily exaggerate the tensions emerging between the United States and the PRC regime, as Beijing is sometimes painted as replacing the old Soviet Union as a new major enemy.[21] Yet, even if we stay well short of this degree of confrontation, we can expect a great many Americans, and the Congressmen who represent them, to be leery of any arrangement where the PRC negotiates a nuclear arsenal equal in size to that of the United States.

Relations between Washington and Beijing have been much less troubled since 1970 than most analysts would have expected in earlier years, at times even becoming cooperative and friendly, and many Americans would assign part of the credit for this to the superiority of the United States in strategic forces.

We can even, as another surprise, expect more than a little Congressional unhappiness at any suggestion that France, and Britain, should be entitled to just as large a nuclear arsenal as the United States, once we drop into the hundreds of weapons. The unhappiness here would be somewhat more formalistic and symbolic, rather than seriously political, on a very simple argument, that Europe in so many ways is 'unifying'. If Europe is now moving toward one currency, and toward a common foreign and defense policy, a Europe without internal borders, how could it be that it would get to 'double-dip', as the United States was allowed only 500 warheads and Russia was allowed a total of 500, but 'Europe' would get a total of 1,000, namely the French 500 plus the British 500?

French spokesmen these days sometimes point to the military instrument, nuclear and conventional, as the one area where integration should be held back, where separate national sovereignties are being preserved, and have to be preserved. Yet, if the rest of European political, economic and social activity were more and more united, any reasonable outside observer, American, Russian, Chinese, or other would be likely to see military unification coming along as a corollary of this.

The idea of a squabble between NATO partners about nuclear force totals will seem far-fetched to most observers, but the point is of course that a world of very low nuclear forces is itself 'far-fetched', that is *very* different in many ways from the world of politics and strategy that we know. The major point here is that this is indeed an unknown world, a world with surprises.

Negotiations may be a way of clarifying the intentions and postures of adversaries in confrontation, reducing the risk of them misunderstanding each other, committing the parties to promises and making it more difficult for anyone to violate their commitments. But the same negotiations may ask nations to accept a legitimacy for inequality that they might have been able to live with quietly, but that they cannot accept so explicitly without a sacrifice of national honor. The Chinese and French and British might find it easier to agree on an ultimate intention to meet each other at zero, as they have indeed done by accepting Article VI of the NPT. But it would be much harder to accept a reduction to 100 when Washington and Moscow had only agreed to reduce to 500.

We can draw two of our problems, two of our possibilities of unpleasant surprise, together here, when we draw in the willingness to disarm of Pakistan and India, and Israel, and Iran and the other countries approaching a nuclear weapons capability, for this combines our second and fourth categories, proliferation and invidious comparison of national honor.

No one can agree to go to zero if there is not an assurance that everyone is going to zero. This is in many ways the easier case, for the ultimate goal is still phrased in terms of equality, with all the difficulty remaining in the transition of getting there.

But a move to lower 'finite' levels of mutual deterrence may indeed have to be the more practical goal, at least for a transitional phase and perhaps for much longer. Yet Russia and America can hardly agree to very much lower numbers of nuclear weapons without considering what the totals are to be for France or China, and the same holds for the totals of all the other 'nth' states. And here we must be prepared for difficulties on both sides, as other states may not be able to accept a formalized American superiority, and Americans may not be able to accept an equality.

Hostility Reopened

The last two categories of the unexpected noted above fold into something more generally undesirable, namely a nourishing of analysis and speculation underscoring a political hostility among the current nuclear weapons states.

No one would claim that nuclear issues determine such hostility or the absence of such hostility all by themselves. What Russians and Americans think of each other changed very much as part of the centrally-determining end of the Cold War, and has had its ups and downs since then. And what Americans and Chinese think of each other has also had its own improvements and worsenings.

Yet the shift to an explicit countervalue targeting focus, and the emergence of arguments about fairness, the two last factors introduced, would together work to make each side think less well of the other. At the minimum, this is again more or less the opposite of what advocates of a denuclearized world would be claiming to expect, one more suggestion of what might more unhappily emerge from the unknown world of low nuclear force levels.

Good News: Forgetting Nuclear Threats?

A very different, perhaps much happier, bit of unexpected news from such a world might be that people in general might pay little or no attention to nuclear weapons and nuclear threats, and in the process achieve a surprising escape from all the negative signals noted above.

Strategists tend to assume that the populations of the cities threatened with nuclear destruction in 'mutual assured destruction' are bound to be upset by this, and/or that they will be upset by scenarios for possible sneak attacks and 'nuclear Pearl Harbors'. Hollywood movies and popular science articles got people excited in the past, and would they not do so again in the future?

Yet one can note several examples from the past where the nuclear threat more or less faded in terms of popular sensitivity. There was a period when Secretary McNamara attempted to justify an American anti-ballistic missiles (ABM) system on the basis of the threat of Chinese Communist nuclear missiles. Yet, as the United States opened up relations with Beijing after 1970, a long period emerged, lasting basically into the late 1990s, where Americans devoted little attention or resentment to this threat.

The French have at times talked of an 'all-azimuth' nuclear strategy, whereby French nuclear forces would presumably not be targeted simply against the Soviet Union, but against every other nuclear-weapon state, on the rational and fair-minded assumption that France has to be ready to retaliate against every possible source of nuclear attack.[22] Yet one never meets a taxi-driver in New York or London who has shown the slightest awareness of, or irritation at, this potential French threat.

More recently, one sometimes hears of strategists encountering fellow Americans who profess not to have realized that we still possess nuclear weapons,[23] who had assumed that total nuclear disarmament had somehow already been accomplished, simply because there was so little in the news about such weapons.

Such blissful ignorance could be entirely good news, easing tensions and avoiding resentments. (It could also at points be bad news in various ways, and this might be left to further analysis elsewhere.) It might simply be noted here as one more illustration of what *might* happen as nuclear forces totals are reduced, and what might not have been predicted or expected by any of us analyzing the trends.

Good News: Internationalizing Nuclear Weapons?

'Realists' about international power politics and nuclear weapons may quickly enough resign themselves to inherent problems with any total nuclear disarmament, such that some basic 'finite' nuclear force would have to be retained at the minimum, lest someone else cheat and suddenly establish a new nuclear monopoly, lest everyone worry about such cheating and be rushing to take preemptive action.

In the realm of the surprising and perhaps unthinkable in a world of much smaller nuclear arsenals, one may thus see a more careful and positive consideration of another 'unthinkable' option, that some or all of such retained weapons be handed over to, or seconded temporarily and contingently to, a higher international authority, most probably the United Nations.[24]

The willingness of Americans and others to hand *ordinary* forces over to such an international body has itself gone up and down in waves of public fashion since the end of the Cold War, with Americans being more positive immediately after the exercise of collective security in the 'Desert Storm' liberation of Kuwait from Iraqi conquest, and then becoming much less positive after the Somalia operation. Some American Congressmen remain adamantly opposed to any such subordination of American forces to UN command, even when Americans were under such command for years in Macedonia.

It would thus be quite a logical leap to see Americans assigning *nuclear* forces to the direction of the UN Security Council or Secretary General. Yet the basic logic that the world will apply at this level if nuclear forces are drastically reduced. These are taxing law and order questions for advocates of world government.

A federated world government along the lines of the League of Nations or the United Nations would seek to prevent all wars just as a domestic system of law and order seeks to prevent all violent crime, by confronting any criminal with sufficient force to keep crime from paying.

Rather than encouraging temptations to cheat, or allowing fears of cheating to loom too large, the force of nuclear weapons retained would thus have to be parallel to the arsenal of weapons retained by the police in even the most crime-free societies, enough to overwhelm, and normally deter, anyone planning to introduce his own weapons as a means of enriching himself.

The nuclear weapons that would be retained under international authority might not have to brandished very much, anymore than the police in Britain normally brandish their weapons potential, as the typical 'Bobby' patrols the community without carrying firearms. But the elementary temptations and fears noted above, as a serious problem for any form of 'nuclear-free world', would dictate that something of a globally responsible nuclear arsenal be retained in order to put such temptations and fears to rest.

Some Conclusions

As we contemplate what the world would look like if nuclear arsenals are drastically reduced, perhaps as a step to their being totally eliminated, the last two more positive possibilities might strike some readers as the most surprising and counter-intuitive of all. Certainly those who are 'realist' interpreters of the anarchic international arena will have difficulty in imagining a world where nuclear weapons are simply forgotten, or are seconded and subordinated to international authority.

Yet the general point here would remain as before, that we know less than we might need to know about what this new nuclear world will be like. There may be pleasant surprises, and as, noted from the outset, there may be many unpleasant surprises, but, in any event, there will almost certainly be surprises.

NOTES

1. Such an analysis is presented in Joseph Rotblat and Vitali Goldanskii, 'The Elimination of Nuclear Arsenals: Is it Desirable? Is it Feasible?', in Francesco Calogero, Marvin Goldberger and Sergei Kapitza (eds.) *Verification: Monitoring Disarmament* (Boulder, CO: Westview Press 1991) pp.205–33.
2. Some of the concerns here are elaborated in Scott Sagan, *The Limits of Safety* (Princeton UP 1993).
3. Albert Wohlstetter, 'The Delicate Balance of Terror', *Foreign Affairs* 37/2 (Jan. 1959) pp.211–34.
4. The basic logic of 'strategic stability' here is outlined in Thomas C. Schelling, *The Strategy of Conflict* (Cambridge, MA: Harvard UP 1960).
5. For a clear presentation of the logic here, see Oskar Morgenstern, *The Question of National Defense* (NY: Random House 1958).
6. On these concerns, see Bruce Blair, *Strategic Command and Control* (Washington DC: Brookings 1985).
7. Such an interpretation is presented in Ludwig Reiners, *The Lamps Went Out in Europe* (NY: Pantheon 1955).
8. This kind of analysis is developed clearly in Thomas Schelling and Morton Halperin, *Strategy and Arms Control* (NY: Twentieth Century Fund 1961).
9. Such arguments about 'fairness' are given an extensive hearing in William Epstein, *The Last Chance* (NY: Free Press 1976).
10. The text of the NPT can be found in United States Arms Control and Disarmament Agency, *Documents on Disarmament, 1968* (Washington DC: USGPO 1969) pp.461–5.
11. See John Redick, 'Factors in the Decision by Argentina and Brazil to Accept the Nonproliferation Regime', in Barry R. Schneider and William L. Dowdy (eds.) *Pulling Back from the Nuclear Brink* (London and Portland, OR: Frank Cass 1998) pp.67–79.
12. For this author's more extended interpretation of nuclear events in South Asia, see George H. Quester, *Nuclear Pakistan and Nuclear India: Stable Deterrent or Proliferation Challenge?* (Carlisle, PA: US Army War College Strategic Studies Inst. 1992).
13. On the classic arguments about extended nuclear deterrence on behalf of NATO during the Cold War, see Bernard Brodie, *Escalation and the Nuclear Option* (Princeton UP 1966).
14. The most-often translated version of this argument is probably that of Pierre Gallois, *The Balance of Terror* (Boston, MA: Houghton Mifflin 1961).
15. A more elaborate version of the argument here is presented in George Quester and Victor Utgoff, 'US Arms Reductions and Nuclear Nonproliferation: The Counterproductive Possibilities', in Brad Roberts (ed.) *US Security in an Uncertain Era* (Cambridge, MA: MIT Press 1993) pp.291–302.
16. For an endorsement of mutual assured destruction, see Wolfgang Panofsky, 'The Mutual Hostage Relationship Between America and Russia', *Foreign Affairs* 52/1 (Oct. 1973) pp.109–18.
17. On the likelihood of moral unease with mutual deterrence, see Fred C. Ikle, 'Can Nuclear Deterrence Last Out the Century?', *Foreign Affairs* 51/2 (Jan. 1973) pp.267–85.
18. Pastoral Letter on *The Challenge of Peace: God's Promise and our Response* (Washington DC: National Conference of Catholic Bishops 1983).
19. For an example, the arguments of Charles Glaser, 'Nuclear Policy Without an Adversary',

International Security, 16/4 (Spring 1992) pp.34–78.

20. A very useful collection of analyses here is presented in John Hopkins and Weixing Hu (eds.) *Strategic Views from the Second Tier* (San Diego, CA: Inst. on Global Conflict and Cooperation 1994).

21. For an example of this kind of prediction, see Richard Bernstein and Ross Munro, *The Coming Conflict With China* (NY: Random House 1997).

22. On French 'doctrine' here, see David S. Yost, 'Nuclear Weapons Issues in France', in Hopkins and Hu (note 20) pp.18–104.

23. For an example, see Robert Manning, 'The Nuclear Age: The Next Chapter', *Foreign Policy* No.109 (Winter 1997–98) pp.70–84.

24. Suggestions for such an internationalization of retained nuclear forces can be found in Richard Garwin, 'Nuclear Weapons for the United Nations', and Vitalii Goldanskii and Stanislav Rodianov, 'An International Nuclear Security Force', in Joseph Rotblat, Jack Steinberger, and Bhalchandrea Udgaonkar (eds.) *A Nuclear-Free World: Desirable? Feasible?* (Boulder, CO: Westview Press 1993) pp.169–80, 181–90, and in Gerard C. Smith, 'Take Nuclear Weapons into Custody', *Bulletin of the Atomic Scientists* 46/10 (Dec. 1990) pp.12–13.

The Role of Nuclear Weapons in US Deterrence Strategy

ROBERT G. JOSEPH

Several years ago, much was being said about how nuclear weapons had run their course with the end of the Cold War. We heard emotional, and in some cases quite eloquent, assertions about the immorality of nuclear weapons and the imperative for the near-term abolition of these weapons. While some of those advocating this course grudgingly granted that the United States continued to require a small nuclear arsenal as long as others possessed nuclear weapons, the hope was that we could blaze the path to complete disarmament by example.

For the most part, there has been little objective analysis of how nuclear weapons contribute to US security, and especially to the deterrence of new threats such as those stemming from the proliferation of weapons of mass destruction. In an effort to address this void, I will examine two of the fundamentals that must be considered in thinking through the role of nuclear weapons in deterrence in the contemporary and future security environment. I will begin with the who – that is those countries that I believe represent either a standing or potential threat to the United States – threats that our nuclear weapons can help to deter. I will then explore the how – that is the practice of deterrence in the circumstances of today, as compared to those of the Cold War. The world has changed fundamentally in the past ten years and will continue to evolve rapidly in the next decade. Our thinking about deterrence must also change.

I would preface my remarks by stating what I believe are two constants. The first is that deterrence remains the first line of defense. The second is that the fundamentals of deterrence have not changed. Effective deterrence continues to depend on both real, not virtual, capabilities and the perception of resolve to respond to aggression. Both of these constants were highlighted in a study that we at the US National Defense University (NDU) co-sponsored with Lawrence Livermore Laboratory last year. This study involved the collective efforts of more than 40 experts in and out of government in exploring the rationale for nuclear weapons in US national security strategy. I will be drawing on this study as well as on some related efforts that we have undertaken at the NDU Center for Counterproliferation

Research that focus on deterring regional adversaries armed with chemical and biological weapons and, in the future, nuclear weapons.

At the Center, we have also conducted a good deal of work on non-state, biological terrorism. This work, however, has led us down the path of consequence management more than deterrence because, quite frankly, I do not know how one deters the type of terrorist that is most likely to use biological weapons for non-traditional objectives. For example, I personally do not believe that the Aum Shinrikyo cult could have been deterred from its 1995 use of sarin in the Tokyo subways. I am confident that nuclear weapons are not part of the equation in these cases, unless there is a link to a state sponsor.

Regarding those states that we need to think about in terms of deterrence, I would begin with Russia. For a variety of reasons, we may wish to ignore or cleverly 'spin' what the Russian leadership says about us and how they see the world, but if we do so, we very well may forgo opportunities to build a better relationship, and we do so at our own peril. Put simply, if we place any stock in what its political and military leaders are saying, Russia considers the United States to be a threat to international stability and, more directly, a threat to its own national security. They say so from former President Yeltsin on down. They have been saying so for several years and on numerous occasions: over NATO enlargement, over Bosnia, more recently over Kosovo and most recently over Chechnya.

In November 1999, Marshal Igor Sergeyev, the Defense Minister, publicly accused the United States of 'seeking to establish control over the North Caucasus' by playing the Afghan card in Chechnya. Sergeyev's argument is that the United States and NATO are trying to weaken Russia by all means, including 'the use of force, disregard for the norms of international law, and *diktat* and high-handedness'. More recently, the Chief of the Russian General Staff suggested that Moscow could expect NATO to use force against former Soviet territory, just as it had in Iraq. In this context, he and others have almost proudly noted the conduct of Russian missile, submarine, and aircraft exercises that to many appear to be patterned after Cold War activities.

Even more disturbing than the words we are hearing is the turbulence and the growing dysfunction of the government in Moscow. Even among those who discount what Russian leaders are saying, most would agree that the strategic uncertainties regarding Russia are staggering. Few would venture to forecast where Russia will be politically in five years or even in one year. Yet most would predict that Russia will continue to possess a large nuclear stockpile for the foreseeable future. While the Russian strategic force level will shrink as a consequence of resource limitations, the overall posture will continue to number warheads in the thousands.

The commander of the Russian strategic missile force recently confirmed what we already knew: Russia intends to rely on its nuclear arsenal for at least the next decade as the primary means to ensure its security. Indicative of this greater reliance on nuclear weapons for both defense planning and declaratory policy is the recent announcement of an across-the-board increase in research and development as well as beginning the production of new tactical weapons. Reportedly, there is also a revised doctrine for the employment of these weapons that lowers the threshold for use in light of the desperate condition of Russia's general purpose forces. This revision would be consistent with Moscow's much earlier reversal on no-first-use.

In sum, Russia is doing what it can to maintain as much nuclear capability as it can, expending very scarce resources on deploying a new mobile missile, keeping heavy multiple, independent re-entry vehicle (MIRVed) missiles in the field, and retaining a massive infrastructure an order of magnitude greater than our own in terms of numbers of personnel and the capability to produce new warheads.

Moving to the next category of states that must be considered in a deterrence context, there is an emerging consensus that countries such as North Korea, Iraq, and Iran – those that our State Department refers to as rogues – represent a growing threat, especially as they acquire weapons of mass destruction. These states define the United States as the enemy without any subtlety or reservation. They believe, quite correctly, that the United States is the major barrier in the way of their strategic goals, whether territorial, political, religious or personal.

While I am somewhat reluctant to group these states together as a single type because of the substantial diversity between and among regimes such as in Baghdad and Pyongyang, they do share characteristics. As a rule, these states are more risk prone than was the former Soviet Union. Moreover, as Keith Payne has pointed out in his work, the conditions that we always valued in our Cold War deterrent relationship, such as effective communication and mutual understandings, are not likely to pertain with these countries. In addition, and again different from the past when the West sought to deter the Warsaw Pact from projecting force outward, these rogue states see as their task deterring the United States from intervening in their regions. As a consequence, the symmetry of the East-West relationship is absent.

Finally, given the West's demonstrated conventional superiority and their knowledge that they will lose in a conventional to conventional fight, the rogues see nuclear, biological and chemical (NBC) weapons as their preferred tool of asymmetric warfare — their best means to achieve victory, either through the threat of large casualties or the actual application of force to accomplish this end. In other words, instead of being weapons of last resort, NBC weapons are becoming weapons of choice, making deterrence essential on our part.

While there does appear to be a consensus within the US defense establishment that the United States must deter this threat, there is no consensus on the role of nuclear weapons in this context. I will return to this point later. Before I do, I will say just a few words about China, the state that in my view poses the greatest strategic uncertainties. Unlike Russia, a country in decline, China is an emerging power, in Asia and perhaps globally. However, like Russia, China's political future is unstable. Whether communism will survive, in what form, or whether there will be a fundamentally different course followed are unanswered questions.

Here again, perhaps the best we can do is note what Chinese leaders are saying as well as what they are doing. Even more forcefully than in Russia, the Chinese are declaring the United States to be a threat to their own national security and to global stability. In an October 1999 interview, their top arms control negotiator, Ambassador Sha, spoke what has become the Party line about the US 'drunk with its own power and technological prowess'. Like many of his colleagues, Sha cites the 1998 bombing of the pharmaceutical plant in Sudan as an act of state terrorism. The 1999 bombing of Yugoslavia is described as an overt illegal act of aggression against a sovereign state. And the bombing of the Chinese embassy in Belgrade is seen as a war crime.

All of this and more, of course, is from a state that has checked every box when it comes to demonstrating rogue behavior, whether that is in the treatment of its own population (from the repression of Tiananmen Square to the persecution of the Fulan Gong), or aggression against its neighbors (such as in Tibet), or support to proliferation programs of states such as Pakistan and Iran, or the use of force to intimidate others (such as firing ballistic missiles near Taiwan). Yet here again, I believe we need to move beyond the acrimonious words, and consider actions.

On modernization, the Chinese determination to develop and deploy a more robust nuclear arsenal is clear. Although Beijing is now citing what it calls provocative US actions, such as talk about deploying light missile defenses, as the reason for their build-up, the scope of the Chinese program reflects a long-standing commitment to improve its nuclear capabilities. The acquisition of MIRV and solid fuel technologies, the deployment of increasingly longer-range mobile missiles, the announcement of the development of neutron warheads, all indicate a broad-based, and well-financed nuclear modernization program.

That the aggressive Chinese modernization program will continue in the future is evidenced by yet another report carried in the US press in

December 1999. China is reportedly beginning construction of a new strategic submarine to carry longer-range missiles based on the design of the Trident W88 warhead. This capability will permit the Chinese to target US nuclear forces for the first time.

The natural question is what do these developments mean for deterrence? Or put differently, how do we need to think about and prepare for deterrence under the new circumstances in each of the three cases outlined above?

Let me start with Russia. Here, the hedge approach is basically sound. Nuclear weapons clearly play a less prominent role than in the past. We have moved beyond the balance of terror as the principal characteristic of our relationship. However, again in a Russian context, in which an unstable and potentially hostile state possesses a large nuclear force, much of how we practiced deterrence in the past remains relevant. For example, deterrence, while more in the background, will continue to be based primarily on the prospect of unacceptable damage from retaliation. Strategic defenses in a deterrent context, as opposed to accidental and unauthorized launch, will not be a major factor given the size and sophistication of the Russian force, even at very reduced levels.

Although the United States could likely go to a somewhat smaller strategic force, our force will still need to be robust and capable, in terms of survivability, effectiveness and responsiveness. For this reason – intercontinental ballistic missiles (ICBMs), sea-launched ballistic missiles (SLBMs), and bombers (all three legs of the triad) – retain their deterrent value for the same reason they did in the past, namely the synergy that provides flexibility to our leadership, that enhances survivability and that complicates defenses.

In the field of arms control, the United States should move beyond the mechanical reductions of the past to a broader engagement encompassing the full spectrum of total nuclear capabilities. At the same time, it is essential to avoid measures that, although advocated in the name of promoting safety and stability, would actually undermine confidence and deterrence. Numerous schemes have been proposed for de-alerting major portions of the US force or for relying on a single leg of the triad in the hope of eliciting a reciprocal response from Russia. Most of these actions are unverifiable and some would engender suspicions and instability.

Most important, the United States must take a long-term view. Politically, we should take care not to perpetuate as official policy the concept of mutual assured destruction with Russia. Promoting this concept, which is grounded in the suspicions and distrust of the Cold War, inevitably has a very corrosive effect on how we perceive each other. If we are to improve our relationship, we need to build on common interests and work on common concerns. For example, the cooperative threat reduction program can make a contribution to our mutual security interests. We must be very aware of our deterrent requirements as a hedge. But we must also aim high and work to change the fundamentals of our relationship.

With regard to the rogues, the prescription is much different. Here, deterrence, and especially deterrence of their use of weapons of mass destruction, is central to our security strategy. But the concept and practice of deterrence in a regional setting bears little resemblance to how we have thought about deterrence in the past. Mutual assured destruction, I would argue, has no relevance with regard to North Korea, Iraq or Iran.

Moreover, effective deterrence must be based not only on the threat of punishment but also on denial, that is the capability to deny the adversary the utility of his weapons of mass destruction. For this reason, counterproliferation capabilities such as improved passive defenses, as well as counterforce means, such as deep underground attack weapons, play a central role in deterrence. Also, and especially in light of the proliferation of long-range missiles, theater and national missile defenses are key.

As mentioned earlier, one issue that is particularly controversial is the role of US nuclear weapons in regional deterrence. Many have simply asserted that we can deter with conventional superiority and that nuclear weapons have no role to play in theater contexts, except possibly for deterring other nuclear weapons. I have seen no evidence to support these assertions.

At NDU we have undertaken several studies of deterrence in a regional setting involving adversaries armed with NBC weapons that shed light on this issue. The results suggest that, in fact, our nuclear weapons are an important component of deterrence of NBC-armed adversaries. One study, conducted primarily through interviews of participants in 'Desert Storm' such as Secretary of Defense Richard B. Cheney, examined deterrence of Iraqi use of chemical and biological weapons (CBW) in the 1991 Gulf War. This is the only real world case study of contemporary deterrence in a regional NBC context. Here are some of the conclusions about deterrence and specifically about the role of our nuclear weapons in deterring Saddam:

- Deterrence of Iraqi CBW did not fail and probably succeeded.

- Nuclear weapons played a conscious role in US deterrence thinking and policy, but most questioned 'feasibility' of actual employment.

- Iraqi leadership believed a US nuclear response to their CBW use was credible.

- Other factors, such as US superior CW-defense capabilities and fear of Israeli retaliation, also contributed to deterrence.

Another effort that has provided insights into deterrence in a regional setting is an extensive gaming effort that we have conducted over the past four years and that now has reached out to more than 2,000 players. The game is very simple. We have the participants work together as an adversary-planning cell, usually in groups of 10 to 12 and usually in a Korean or Southwest Asian scenario. The planners are given chemical and biological capabilities similar to those we believe these countries actually possess, and they are told to develop a plan to achieve specific political or military objectives, such as breaking a coalition or disrupting the flow of US and allied forces into theater.

At the end of the game, we ask the players what factors most influenced their willingness to use chemical and biological weapons and what capabilities on the US side were the most effective deterrent to their use of these weapons. The data collected indicate several capabilities that work together to strengthen deterrence. These include: CBW detection and warning, improved protective equipment, superior intelligence, and theater and national missile defenses. By far, the most important single capability that enhances deterrence of NBC use as cited by the game participants is the US nuclear force.

Moving to the third and most difficult case, China, I believe this challenge lies somewhere in-between Russia and the rogues. Clearly, US nuclear weapons will remain central in both hedging against uncertainties and, at times, deterring aggressive Chinese actions, such as against Taiwan. However, there are many unknowns in the deterrence equation with China. As a nation, we will need to address some of the central questions that we have already answered for the other two deterrent cases.

Should we, for instance, accept a mutual assured destruction (MAD) relationship with China? Unless we act now, we will be accepting MAD *de facto* as China modernizes its nuclear force. This appears to be the course. In early December 1999, the White House press spokesman stated that he is not worried about China's development of a new ballistic missile submarine. The reason: the United States has 'a clearly superior nuclear force'. In fact, we should be concerned about Chinese nuclear modernization because it is directed at us. Soon the Chinese will be able to target all major US population centers. At a minimum, we need to ask ourselves some of the fundamental questions. What are our options with regard to China? Can we build a sufficiently robust strategic defense capability against a growing Chinese offensive force? What are the implications of these questions for deterrence and for the political relationship we would like to build with Beijing? It is only after we have thought through these and other questions that we can arrive at sound judgements on deterrence policy and requirements for China.

Conclusion

I would emphasize three points that I believe will be essential to deterrence in the future. The first is the requirement to retain a nuclear weapons infrastructure that is sufficiently robust to maintain current forces and sufficiently adaptive to provide new capabilities when required. This will include both new platforms and, most likely, new warheads. The United States is in the deterrence business for the long term and we must devote the required resources to develop and deploy the necessary capabilities. Here, one of the greatest challenges will be sustaining personnel competence in nuclear matters – from weapons design to operational expertise in the field.

Second, we need to recognize that defenses are an increasingly important part of deterrence. We must not let outdated, Cold War concepts and treaties, such as the ABM Treaty, stand in the way of acquiring the denial capabilities we need to deter the most urgent threats we face today.

And finally, and staying with the arms control point, we need to be realistic about the prospects and contributions that arms control can make. Most of all, we should follow the code of 'doing no harm'. It was this code that the Comprehensive Test Ban Treaty would have clearly violated by undercutting our deterrent forces in the future for all three cases that I have identified.

Deterrence and Conventional Military Forces

GARY L. GUERTNER

The search for a US national security strategy periodically opens major policy debates that push policy makers in new, sometimes revolutionary directions. The collapse of the Soviet Union and the end of the Cold War have given rise to a national debate unmatched since the end of World War II. Dramatic changes in the international system have forced Americans to reevaluate old strategies and look for new focal points amidst the still unsettled debris of the bipolar world. At issue is the role of the United States and its capabilities to defend and promote its national interests in a new environment where threats are both diffuse and uncertain and where conflict is inherent yet unpredictable.

The degree of uncertainty requires flexibility in US military strategy and significant departures from Cold War concepts of deterrence. This contribution examines new options for deterrence. Its primary thesis is that new conditions in both the international and domestic environments require a dramatic and more accelerated shift from a nuclear dominant deterrent to one that is based on conventional forces. The study identifies the theories and strategies of nuclear deterrence that can also be applied to modern conventional forces in a multi-polar world.

One obstacle to analysis of that transfer is semantic. The simultaneous rise of the Cold War and the nuclear era produced a body of literature and a way of thinking in which deterrence became virtually synonymous with nuclear weapons. In fact, deterrence has always been pursued through a mix of nuclear and conventional forces. The force mix changed throughout the Cold War in response to new technology, anticipated threats, and fiscal constraints. There have been, for example, well-known cycles in both US and Soviet strategies when their respective strategic concepts evolved from nuclear-dominant deterrence (the 'massive retaliation' of Dwight D. Eisenhower and its short-lived counterpart under Nikita Khrushchev), to the more balanced deterrent (John F. Kennedy to Ronald Reagan) of flexible response, which linked conventional forces to a wide array of nuclear capabilities in a 'seamless web' of deterrence that was 'extended' to US allies in the North Atlantic Treaty Organization (NATO).

Early proponents of nuclear weapons tended to view nuclear deterrence as a self-contained strategy, capable of deterring threats across a wide spectrum of threat. By contrast, the proponents of conventional forces have always argued that there are thresholds below which conventional forces pose a more credible deterrent. Moreover, there will always be nondeterrable threats to US interests that will require a response, and that response, if military, must be commensurate with the levels of provocation. A threat to use nuclear weapons against a Third World country, for instance, would put political objectives at risk because of worldwide reactions and the threat of escalation beyond the theater of operations.

The end of the Cold War has dramatically altered the 'seamless web' of deterrence and has decoupled nuclear and conventional forces. Nuclear weapons have a declining political-military utility below the threshold of deterring a direct nuclear attack against the territory of the United States. As a result, the post-Cold War period is one in which stability and the deterrence of war are likely to be measured by the capabilities of conventional forces. Ironically, the downsizing of US and allied forces is occurring simultaneously with shifts in the calculus of deterrence that call for conventional domination of the force mix.

Downsizing was driven by legitimate domestic and economic issues, but it also needs continuous strategic guidance and rationale. The political dynamics of defense cuts, whether motivated by the desire to disengage from foreign policy commitments or by the economic instinct to save the programs in the defense budget richest in jobs, threaten the development of a coherent post-Cold War military strategy. This analysis identifies strategic options for a credible deterrence against new threats to US interests. Most can be executed by conventional forces, and present conditions make a coherent strategy of general, extended conventional deterrence feasible.

Critics of conventional deterrence argue that history has demonstrated its impotence. By contrast, nuclear deterrence of the Soviet threat arguably bought 45 years of peace in Europe. The response to this standard critique is threefold. First, conditions now exist (and were demonstrated through air and land power in the Persian Gulf War and in Kosovo) in which the technological advantages of US conventional weapons and doctrine are so superior to the capabilities of all conceivable adversaries that their deterrence value against direct threats to US interests is higher than at any period in American history.

Second, technological superiority and operational doctrine allow many capabilities previously monopolized by nuclear strategy to be readily transferred to conventional forces. For example, conventional forces now have a combination of range, accuracy, survivability, and lethality that allows them to execute strategic attacks, simultaneously or sequentially, across a wide spectrum of targets that include counter force, command and control (including leadership), and economic elements.

Third, critics of conventional deterrence have traditionally set impossible standards for success. Over time, any form of deterrence may fail. The United States will always confront some form of nondeterrable threat. Moreover, deterrence is a perishable commodity. It wears out and must periodically be revived. Failures of deterrence provide the opportunity to demonstrate the price of aggression, rejuvenate the credibility of deterrence (collective or unilateral), and establish a new period of stability. In other words, conventional deterrence can produce long cycles of stability instead of the perennial or overlapping intervals of conflict that would be far more likely in the absence of a carefully constructed US (and allied) conventional forces capability.

A Deterrent Based on Conventional Forces

Conventional deterrence has a future, but one very different from its past, in which it was subordinated to nuclear threats and strategic nuclear theory. The United States now faces a multi-polar international political system that may be destabilized by a proliferation of armed conflict and advanced weaponry. To secure stability, security, and influence in this new world order, the United States can use the military prowess it demonstrated in the Persian Gulf War and in Kosovo to good advantage. Using that force effectively, however, or threatening to use it, requires the formulation of a coherent strategy of 'general extended conventional deterrence' and the prudent planning of general purpose forces that are credible and capable of underwriting a new military strategy.

An additional paradox confronting conventional forces in an era of peacekeeping operations is the dual requirements for maintaining technological superiority as a vital force multiplier, while engaging a growing number of conflicts at the low end of the spectrum.[1] Such conflicts, if Kosovo is a typical example, give adversaries ample opportunities to exploit asymmetric strategies if and when the US and its allies cannot react swiftly. Kosovo also illustrates how broadly we must define conventional forces, taking into account a range from precision guided munitions to the non-lethal weapons employed for the first time by US forces assigned to Kosovo forces (KFOR).

Neither proponents nor critics should judge this analysis in isolation. Conventional deterrence cannot succeed unless it is reinforced by supporting policies and concepts. The strategic concepts in the National Military Strategy that appear to have the greatest synergistic value in support of conventional deterrence are:

FIGURE 1
CONVENTIONAL DETERRENCE AND INTERNATIONAL STABILITY

Period of Stability	Deterrence Failure	Stability Restored OR	Instability Spreads
• Military technology advances	• Crisis or war	• Aggression is countered	• Aggression succeeds
			• Deterrence fails
• Weapons proliferate	• Collective security	• Conventional forces and doctrine demonstrate capabilities	• Utility of aggression demonstrated
• Political and economic conflicts flare	• Collective defense	• Conventional deterrence revitalized	• Period of instability extended in scope and duration
• Incentives for war increase	• Unilateral action		
• Risk of miscalculation increases		• New period of stability begins	
		• US interests protected	• US interests at risk
• Deterrence fails			

- technological superiority;
- collective security;
- forward presence;
- strategic agility; and theater defenses.[2]

Technological Superiority

Recent reductions in the overall force structure will make the force-multiplying effects of technological superiority more important than ever. Space-based sensors, defense-suppression systems, 'brilliant weapons,' and stealth technologies give true meaning to the concept of force multipliers. This broad mix of technologies forecast in *Joint Vision 2010* can make conventional forces decisive provided they are planned and integrated into an effective doctrine and concept of operations.

The conflicts most likely to involve the United States will be confrontations with less capable states that have trouble employing their forces and their technology in effective combined arms operations. As Anthony Cordesman has concluded in his assessment of the 1991 Persian Gulf War, the US can cut its force structure and still maintain a decisive military edge over most threats in the Third World. It can exploit the heritage of four decades of arming to fight a far more sophisticated and combat-ready enemy so that it can fight under conditions where it is outnumbered or suffers from significant operational disadvantages.[3]

Exploiting technology to get economies of force will require investments where the payoff in battlefield lethality is greatest. Given the threats that US forces are most likely to confront in regional contingencies, these technologies will include:

- battle management resources for real-time integration of sensors-command-control and weapon systems that make enemy forces transparent and easily targeted;

- mobility of conventional forces to fully exploit technological superiority and battlefield transparency;

- smart conventional weapons with range and lethality; and

- component upgrades for existing delivery platforms to avoid costly generational replacements.

This means limited procurement of new tactical fighters, tanks, bombers, submarines, or other platforms that were originally conceived to counter a modernized Soviet threat.

Technology that leads to unaffordable procurement threatens the US military with force multipliers of less than net decreases in combat-capable forces can best be avoided through combinations of selective upgrading and selective low-rate procurement. Bureaucratic pressures to produce three new tactical fighters represent the antithesis of how to build cost-effective force multipliers.

Technological superiority will also depend on concurrent political strategies. Technology is a double-edged sword; it can act as a force multiplier, but the laws of science apply equally to potential US adversaries. Multilateral support for the nonproliferation of both nuclear and critical conventional military technologies can be an equally effective means for preempting threats to US interests and for underwriting conventional deterrence.

Collective Security

Collective security has become explicitly incorporated in *The National Military Strategy*. It is broadly defined to include both collective security (activities sanctioned by the United Nations [UN]) and collective defense arrangements (formal alliances such as an enlarged NATO). These are linked informally in what could, if promoted by the United States, form transregional security linkages – a 'seamless web' of collective action.[4]

The potential value of collective security to conventional deterrence is difficult to quantify because it requires the United States to link its security to the capabilities and political will of others. Its potential must always be balanced against the risk that collective action may require significant limitations on unilateral action. Nevertheless, there are three compelling reasons for the United States to embrace collective security.[5]

- Allies or coalition partners are essential for basing or staging the range of capabilities required to fully exploit technologically superior forces against a regional hegemony.

- The American public shows little enthusiasm for an active role as the single, global   superpower. Collective deterrence is politically essential for sharing not only the military burden, but also the increasingly salient political and fiscal responsibilities.

- Patterns of collective action, as demonstrated in the Persian Gulf War and in the Balkans, give conventional deterrence credibility and capabilities that the United States can no longer afford or achieve on its own. Even though collective action and shared capabilities may limit US freedom of action, these limits are reassuring to others and may contribute more to stability than attempts by the world's only superpower to unilaterally impose deterrence – nuclear or conventional.

Forward Presence

The post-Cold War shift in US military strategy from large-scale forward deployments of military forces to limited or intermittent forward presence is linked to the credibility of both conventional deterrence and collective security.[5]

US forces abroad will continue to be viewed as the most visible symbols of US resolve and commitment to regional stability. They are vital components of both short- and long-range stability because they:

- demonstrate US leadership, commitment, and capabilities for collective security, collective defense, and peacekeeping operations;

- contribute to the preservation of regional power balances and provide disincentives for the nationalization of regional defense policies and of arms competitions; and

- contribute to the containment of security obstacles that, absent a US presence, could disrupt regional economic integration and political union, both vital components of long-term regional stability.

The forward presence of US military forces as part of collective security or collective defense regimes has a deterrent value in excess of its immediate military capabilities, provided that these symbols of US commitment are backed by the strategic agility to bring credible military force to bear at decisive points and at decisive times in a crisis.

Strategic Agility

Strategic agility is a generic concept that reflects the dramatic changes in Cold War forward-deployment patterns that fixed US forces on the most threatened frontiers in Germany and Korea. Old planning assumptions have given way to new requirements to meet diffuse regional contingencies. Simply stated, US forces will be assembled by their rapid movement from wherever they are to wherever they are needed. Strategic agility requires mobile forces and adaptive planning for a diverse range of options. Many of these options signal US commitment and demonstrate military capabilities short of war. Joint exercises, UN peacekeeping missions, and even humanitarian/disaster relief operations provide opportunities to display power projection capabilities and global reach despite reduced forward deployment of forces.

Theater Ballistic Missile Defenses

Nuclear and chemical weapons proliferation make theater air and antitactical ballistic missile defenses important components of conventional deterrence. The next states that are likely to acquire nuclear arms are under radical regimes that are openly hostile to US interests (North Korea, Libya, Iran, and Iraq). The success of such regional powers in creating even a small nuclear umbrella under which they could commit aggression would represent a serious challenge to US global strategy.[6]

Theater defenses in support of conventional deterrence need not be a part of the grander objectives of the Strategic Defense Initiative or its most recent variant, Global Protection Against Limited Strikes (GPALS). The layered, space-based weapons architecture of these costly systems seems, at best, technologically remote and, at worst, a vestige of the Cold War. What is needed in the near term is a global, space-based early warning, command and control network that is linked to modernized, mobile, land-based theater defense systems (Patriot follow-on, Theater High-Altitude Area Defense [THAAD] or sea-based interceptors designed for greater defense of both military forces and countervalue targets such as cities).[7]

Theater Strategic Targeting with Conventional Forces

Uncertainties about nondeterrable nuclear threats make it all the more imperative that the United States also have credible warfighting options. Nuclear preemption prior to an attack is not plausible, and there are uncertainties as to whether any president or his coalition partners would authorize a response in kind, even if the enemy used nuclear weapons first. More plausible are the range of conventional options afforded by modern, high-tech weapons that have a theater strategic capability for both denial and punishment missions. The broad outline of a conventional deterrence strategy would include:

- conventional preemption of the nuclear/chemical infrastructure and key command and control nodes to deny or disrupt an attack (deterrence by denial);

- threats of conventional escalation to countervalue targets (economic) if nuclear weapons are used (deterrence by punishment);

- threats to seize enemy territory (deterrence by punishment);

- countervalue retaliation by conventional forces if deterrence and preemption fail (deterrence by punishment); and

- theater antitactical missile and air defenses (deterrence by denial).

The imperfect capability of deterrence by denial (even with nuclear weapons) and the unknowable responses to threats of retaliation and punishment leave theater antitactical ballistic missile defenses as the last line of defense for US and coalition forces. On balance, conventional deterrence that combines attempts to dissuade, capabilities to neutralize or capture, credible threats to retaliate, and the ability to defend is more credible against regional powers than nuclear threats. Together, these capabilities dramatically reduce the coercive potential of Third World nuclear programs. This does not mean, however, that nuclear forces have no role to play in the future of deterrence.

The Role of Nuclear Weapons in a Deterrent Dominated by Conventional Forces

The National Military Strategy states that the purpose of nuclear forces is 'to deter the use of weapons of mass destruction and to serve as a hedge against the emergence of an overwhelming conventional threat.[8]

The dilemma confronting the United States is still the same classic problem that confronted strategists throughout the Cold War. Nuclear weapons fulfill their declared deterrence function only if they are never used. Yet, if everyone knows that they will never be used, they lack the credibility to deter. The most credible means to resolve this dilemma is through a combination of declaratory policies and military capability that emphasizes the warfighting capabilities of conventional forces with strategic reach.

There is, however, a potential paradox of success if aggressive Third World leaders believe that only weapons of mass destruction can offset US advantages in conventional military power. Under such circumstances, theater nuclear weapons can have important signaling functions that communicate new risks and introduce greater costs for nuclear aggression that inflicts high casualties on US forces or on allied countervalue targets.

Nuclear signaling can take the form of declarations by the president or the Department of Defense (DoD) that US ships deploying to a hostile theater of operations have been refitted with nuclear weapons carried by dual-capable aircraft (DCA) and Tomahawk Land Attack Missiles (TLAM).[9] Deployment options alone can play a critical role in the strategic calculus of aggressors who possess uncommitted nuclear capabilities.

The role of strategic nuclear forces is also directly related to the problems of reorienting the National Military Strategy from a global to a regional focus. The first problem is determining the force structure after the combined reductions of the Strategic Arms Reduction Treaty (START).

The combined results will be dramatic cuts in US strategic forces from some 12,000 warheads to 3,500, or even as few as 1,000. These cuts are prudent responses to the military collapse of the Russian Federation and give the United States and its allies a long-sought opportunity to pull back from the nuclear brink where they so often found themselves during the Cold War. Moreover, these reductions are consistent with obligations under the Nuclear Non-Proliferation Treaty (NPT).

The credibility of US support for nonproliferation will also be affected by the declaratory policies and targeting strategy for a smaller strategic nuclear force structure. In their current form, nuclear declaratory policies are excessive and favor a nuclear force structure that is not well suited for credible deterrence. The United States could be accused of a double standard in proclaiming the value of nuclear weapons at the same time that it was asking others to forswear them.

In the case of the Russian Federation, US targeting policy should be muted. Prudence dictates that advantage be taken of every opportunity for mutual reductions of force levels and confidence-building measures such as lower alert rates, improved command and control structures, and cooperative steps to improve the safety of nuclear storage, transportation, and destruction procedures.[10]

Russia will remain a nuclear power with a potential to threaten the United States and its allies. On the other hand, it is no longer the center of a hostile global movement or the leader of a powerful military alliance threatening Europe with overwhelming force deep in its own territory. Russian behavior is shaped more by its need for Western aid and technology than by US military capabilities. It is difficult to conceive credible scenarios in which even the most reactionary Great Russian nationalist could find in nuclear weapons the tools that could be used against the West in preplanned ways to coerce concessions or that might tempt revisionist leaders to adopt reckless and inflexible positions. The United States will and should, along with its British and French allies, retain nuclear options, but it is premature in the extreme to plan robust nuclear attacks against the 'force projection assets' of a state that is struggling for democracy and economic reforms.[11]

Even though the United States may be a benevolent superpower, the political impact of global nuclear targeting is more likely to stimulate rather than deter nuclear proliferation. An alternative set of declaratory policies that are consistent with nonproliferation includes commitments to deep cuts in nuclear forces coupled with a *defensive* strategy of direct retaliation against nuclear attacks on US territory. Direct retaliation is one of the few credible missions for strategic nuclear forces in the post-Cold War world. Extending deterrence should be a function of conventional forces.

Global retargeting of nuclear forces is an unfortunate concept that is more likely to put US interests at risk in the long run. Marshal of Aviation Yevgenii I. Shaposhnikov, former C-in-C of the Commonwealth of Independent States' Armed Forces, struck a more positive image in his correct observation that retargeting frightens people. It is better, he said, to discuss 'non-targeting', which lowers the level of alert to 'zero flight assignments of missiles'.[12]

The Marshal's formulations were too vague to serve as the basis of national policy. Nevertheless, his point should not be dismissed. The objectives of national military strategy are more likely to be achieved through the *implicit* flexibility to respond to nuclear aggression from any source rather than *explicit* declarations of global nuclear targeting. Many regional crises may be precipitated by the proliferation of nuclear weapons and ballistic missiles.

US strategy will, therefore, require a delicate balance lest it give incentives to that very threat. A reassuring posture, in the eyes of regional actors and global partners, will require reexamination and 'denuclearization' of deterrence in a new multipolar world.

Finally, and above all, this contribution's primary purpose has been to recommend the option of using modern conventional forces for strategic purposes. A reliance on offensive nuclear weapons carries enormous risks that have already brought the United States and its allies to the brink of war during several cold war crises. The American public has every right to expect that the Cold War's principal legacy of danger not be deliberately extended into the new millennium.

A conventional dominant deterrent will require full emancipation from Cold War thinking. As Fred Ikle wisely noted, strategic thought in some quarters 'remains locked into place by dated nuclear arsenals', and these forces remain tied to imaginative scenarios that 'persist, like a genetic defect'.[13]

Freeing US military strategy from its nuclear past will require deeper cuts in the existing strategic nuclear force structure and in strategic defense spending. START II was a dramatic step, but one that when fully implemented will leave the United States with nearly as many strategic nuclear warheads as it deployed in 1970, the period when serious efforts were just beginning for negotiated limits on Soviet and US nuclear forces.[14]

Deeper cuts will be required to win congressional support for a conventional force structure that is capable of meeting the regional contingencies in the new national military strategy. Failure to clearly address how and why the US force structure must change will result in an impotent mix of nuclear and conventional forces that will neither deter, nor be capable of meeting threats to US interests.

NOTES

The views expressed here are those of the author and do not necessarily reflect the official policy or position of the Department of the Army, the Department of Defense, or the US government. This is an update of an article, same title, published by the US Army War College, Strategic Studies Institute (Carlisle Barracks, PA, May 1992).

1. This paradox for US military strategy is described in *Strategic Assessment 1999*, Chapter 17, 'Conventional Operations and Warfare: A New Era Ahead?' (Inst. for National Strategic Studies, National Defense Univ., Washington DC 1999).
2. These strategic concepts are drawn from *The National/Military Strategy 1992*, released by the chairman of the Joint Chiefs of Staff in Jan. 1992. Some have been narrowed in scope for ease of analysis. For example, the NMS lists strategic deterrence and defense as one of the four foundations on which US strategy is built. This essay narrows this strategic concept to conventional deterrence and theater defense. These concepts have also been integrated in greater detail in *Joint Vision 2010*.
3. Anthony H. Cordesman, 'Compensating For Smaller Forces: Adjusting Ways and Means Through Technology' (Paper presented at the Third Annual Strategy Conference, US Army War College, Strategic Studies Inst., Carlisle Barracks, PA, 14 Feb. 1992) p.2.
4. For a detailed assessment of collective security and US strategy, see Inis Claude Jr, Sheldon Simon, and Douglas Stuart, *Collective Security in Asia and Europe* (Carlisle Barracks, PA: US Army War College, Strategic Studies Inst., 2 March 1992). Ironically, the administration's pledge to support growing UN peacekeeping activities is under attack by members of Congress because of a long-standing agreement that makes the United States responsible for 30 per cent of the cost of every operation. Japan and the West Europeans could conceivably relieve part of the perceived inequity, but Congress should also examine these costs in the larger context of collective security and global stability. See Don Oberdorfer, 'Lawmakers Balk at Peacekeeping's Cost', *Washington Post*, 4 March 1992, p.A-17.
5. *The National Military Strategy* describes forward presence operations to include forward stationed troops, forces afloat, periodic rotational deployments, access and storage agreements, military exercises, security and humanitarian assistance, port visits, and military-co-military contacts.

6. Leonard S. Spector, 'Deterring Regional Threats from Nuclear Proliferation' (Paper presented at the Third Annual Strategy Conference, US Army War College, Strategic Studies Inst., Carlisle Barracks, PA, 14 Feb. 1992) p.31 and Appendix A.

7. The growing interest in a flexible, sea-based ballistic missile defense system was outlined by Ambassador Henry Cooper in an address to NATO Parliamentarians at the American Enterprise Institute, Washington DC, 4 Feb. 2000.

8. *The National Military Strategy 1992*, p.13.

9. President George Bush's unilateral initiatives in Sept. 1991 eliminated ground-launched tactical nuclear weapons and withdrew them from surface ships and submarines. Some sea-based weapons are scheduled for destruction. Others are in storage whence they can be redeployed for the 'signaling' purposes advocated here.

10. These latter steps are well under way. Congress allocated $400 million to assist Russian efforts to transport, store, and destroy nuclear weapons, and on 26 March 1992 the State Department announced the appointment of Retired Maj. Gen. William F. Burns, former director of the US Arms Control and Disarmament Agency, to head the US delegation on Safety, Security, and Dismantlement of Nuclear Weapons (SSD Talks). Moscow has agreed to US assistance in the production of containers for missile material from dismantled nuclear weapons, conversion of rail cars for secure transport, construction of storage facilities, training in nuclear accident response, accounting procedures, and ultimate disposition of enriched uranium and plutonium. See Department of State Press Release, 26 March 1992.

11. Open discussions of nuclear targeting in the press were followed by equally controversial reporting of threat scenarios that were developed in the Office of the Chairman of the Joint Chiefs of Staff. These scenarios included a hypothetical NATO counterattack if Russia invaded Lithuania. There is virtually no support in NATO or in the US Congress for such a course of action. The scenario does, however, raise the question of what the United States should do in the event of a Russian-initiated civil war to reunite the former Soviet Union. Russian nationalists could indeed threaten nuclear retaliation against Western intervention. History suggests, however, that Western response would be political and economic, but not military, thus making nuclear threats irrelevant. 'Threat' scenarios are discussed by Barton Gellman, 'Pentagon War Scenario Spotlights Russia', *Washington Post*, 20 Feb.1992, p.A-1.

12. Marshal Yevgenii I. Shaposhnikov, interview in *Red Star*, 22 Feb. 1992, pp.1–3. Quoted in Foreign Broadcast Information Service, *Central Eurasia*, 24 Feb. 1992 (FBIS-SOV-92-036), p.8.

13. Quoted in Michael J. Mazarr, 'Nuclear Weapons After the Cold War', *The Washington Quarterly* 15 (Summer 1992), p.198.

14. In 1970, a period when the Soviets achieved strategic nuclear parity with the United States, US strategic nuclear warheads numbered 3,780. Data compiled from *The Military Balance*, 1969–1972 editions (London: Int. Inst. for Strategic Studies). Ironically, the Strategic Arms Limitation Talks (SALT I) initiated by President Richard M. Nixon in 1969 resulted, over time, in a fourfold increase in US strategic nuclear warheads.

Terrorism in the 21st Century: Reassessing the Emerging Threat

DANIEL S. GRESSANG IV

In the President's *National Security Strategy*,[1] terrorism is presented as one of the most pressing and disturbing threats to both the interests and national security of the United States. The threat of terrorist attack against Americans abroad is quite obviously at odds with the administration's stated goal of creating and maintaining a peaceful and secure international environment. But terrorism is not seen simply as a threat, it is a growing threat. The possibility that terrorists would consider using weapons of mass destruction (WMD) – chemical, biological, or nuclear devices – against America and American interests has emerged in US policy as a leading concern. To guard against these threats, the United States has aggressively pursued a policy of deterrence and coordinated response, designed to minimize the severity of terrorist actions while also fostering a spirit of international cooperation against terrorism. The intent, quite clearly, is to create, through unilateral and multilateral actions, an environment which is not conducive to terrorist activities.

More disturbing still, however, is the threat that terrorists would not only use weapons of mass destruction, but that the use of such weapons would take place within US borders. The *National Security Strategy* clearly sees this as a possibility in the coming years, labeling the threat of terrorist WMD use as a critical emerging threat at home. Presidential Decision Directive 62, signed in May 1998, directly addresses this possibility in outlining the roles and responsibilities of various federal agencies in response to terrorist WMD use.[2]

In addition, the Domestic Terrorism Program seeks to integrate federal agencies' capabilities to provide for timely, effective, and appropriate consequence management in the event of WMD use in the United States. Subsequent policies and programs, including the creation of several incident response teams, all emphasize this desire for efficient and effective response to major incidents of terror.

The question remains, however, of whether these plans and programs will serve as an effective counter to the terrorist threat. Questions remain concerning timeliness of responses, time lags in recognizing outbreaks of illness as acts of terrorism, distribution of and access to appropriate antidotes and treatments, and other issues related to response timeliness and appropriateness. Despite the critical need to address the broad range of issues subsumed under the crisis response and consequence management rubrics, as these are, all such questions emphasize a series of plans, procedures, and programs to be implemented after terrorists strike. However important they may be, these questions are striking in their consistency. All presume, intentionally or unintentionally, and are predicated upon the notion that the initiative rests with the terrorist.

Despite the reactive nature of current discussions and debate, the *National Security Strategy* clearly outlines an intent to prevent and deter terrorist attacks. Each goal, prevention and deterrence, presupposes government initiative. That initiative can be realized through the creation of a climate unfavorable to terrorist activities, through aggressive law enforcement which could create an expectation of futility of terrorist action, through prompt and aggressive sanctions – including military sanctions – applied to those responsible, or in other ways. In an effort to craft a preventive or deterrent strategy, however, knowledge of the adversary is critical, for it alone allows for the development of a tailored strategy designed to address the essential elements of contention or the most significant areas of vulnerability. This study seeks to foster such consideration by first outlining prevailing perceptions of the terrorist threat. From this examination, a set of common perceptions and beliefs is distilled and considered in the context of terrorism as a process. In the end, this analysis offers a restatement of the emerging threat of terrorism, one stripped of the perceptual biases which foster an exaggerated view of the terrorist threat.

Before the threat, or perceptions of the threat, can be considered, however, a brief discussion of what constitutes terrorism is in order. One can find literally hundreds of competing definitions of terrorism, all with a measure of truth and substance, but all also reflecting more or less the biases and opinions of each definition's author. For the present discussion, terrorism is held to be violence, or the threat of violence, intentionally directed against non-combatants for political, social, or economic reasons other than material gain. Furthermore, this violence or threat of violence is intended to communicate some message to an audience much wider than the immediate victims of the act. The act used to transmit the message, additionally, has a significant dramatic component, generally to create, instill, or perpetuate a perception in that audience of fear. The violence may be sponsored by governmental authorities and may be conducted by the duly constituted agencies and services of a government, but may also be authored by groups of individuals working in concert without the enjoyment of legal status or protection. Finally, no specific ideological, theological, or philosophical bases are assumed, since the intent to create or foster a sense of fear beyond the immediate victim remains the principal *raison d'être* for the violent act or threat.

Terrorism's Popular Perspective

Popular portrayals of the emerging terrorist threat offer nightmare visions of almost unfathomable death and destruction. The fanatical religious or millennial extremist, unconcerned with worldly consequences of his act, is often offered as the driving force for violence. Even more frightening, the potential for terrorist use of mass casualty weapons – particularly chemical, biological, radiological, or nuclear – offers a vision of almost unimaginable horror.[3]

Even more frightening, perhaps, is the way in which recent events seem to match what has been, until now, well within the realm of fiction. Aum Shinrikyo, in using sarin nerve gas in the Tokyo subway system in 1995, seems to have finally broken the barrier to large-scale use of mass casualty weapons. Since then, we have become more sensitized to reports of radical, extremist, and fringe groups or individuals seeking to acquire chemical, biological, radiological, or nuclear materials. Adding to these fears is the apparent increase in far-right militancy and violence, particularly within our own country. Not only have we now seen the first terrorist spectacular on American soil, but also an apparent wave of individual attacks by adherents of far-right groups.

The mass media is not alone in offering chilling portraits of the potential of WMD terrorism, since much of the current academic literature on the recent evolution and future of terrorism offer many of the same perspectives, visions, and predictions. That perspective extends, additionally, to the government, with Congressional debates and hearings, policy speeches, and publicly released reports and testimony emphasizing actual or needed preparations for responding to such nightmare threats.[4]

Are these perspectives an accurate reflection of the threat and are they useful for considering deterring terrorism? Have such visions offered a view of terrorism, and the threat it poses for the United States, sufficient to design and implement an effective deterrence strategy? Or have we inadvertently allowed ourselves to focus on diffuse and uncertain possibilities, particularly worst-case scenarios, in such a ways as to bias or limit our assessments and their effectiveness?

In this essay, I will suggest that the latter may well be the case: that we have become, over the last 30 years, so focused on the structural aspects of terrorist organizations and so enamored of their professed ideologies and theologies, that we have lost sight of the essential and most fundamental driving force of terrorist action – the desire to gain and maintain influence. I will also suggest that re-emphasizing this communicative and suasive aspect of the terrorists' *raison d'être* will offer a more productive set of insights into the emerging terrorist threat.

Popular Media

Much of the popular media, including fiction and non-fiction, seem to emphasize stereotypic perspectives. Whether that portrayal is of the fanatical Islamic suicide bomber, gleefully driving to his death, or the determined secularist out for revenge at any cost, we are offered a steady diet of stereotyped or generalized characters and situations. Usama bin Laden is not simply an Arab, a Saudi, or a Muslim, but a fanatical fundamentalist, an ostracized and exiled radical hell-bent on causing violence to America, its citizens, and all other elements of the western world. We see aspects of his heritage, beliefs, and culture and emphasize those things we find different from ourselves.[5] We assume, it frequently seems, that because they behave in ways we disagree with that the explanation for their actions can be found in those differences. We seem somehow unwilling or unable to see many foreign terrorists as humans like ourselves.

And when we look among ourselves, to the Unabomber, to Timothy McVeigh, to Terry Nichols, we see perhaps too much of ourselves. We see people like us, with similar backgrounds and histories, with shared cultural heritage, sometimes with the same general political or religious leanings. Yet we also see behavior far beyond the norms we have come to expect. While the differences we see between ourselves and foreign terrorists often serve to comfort us, the similarities we see between ourselves and many domestic groups shock and frighten us.

Popular literature, including many media portrayals, heighten the differences we find in terrorists abroad and search for – some might say manufacture – similar distinctions for terrorists here. We often see, as a consequence, images and descriptions of the shocking – religious fanaticism, millennial or apocalyptic cults, and the potential for use of mass casualty weapons. We see terrorist spectaculars authored by those who seem radically different from ourselves:

- the October 1983 suicide bombing of the Marine Barracks in Beirut, Lebanon, by Islamic radicals;

- the December 1988 downing of Pan Am Flight 103 over Lockerbie, Scotland, coupled with the downing of UTA flight 772 the following year, by agents of a radical Arab state;

- the February 1993 bombing of the World Trade Center in New York City by Islamic radicals;

- the March 1995 sarin gas attack in Tokyo by a Japanese cult;

- the April 1995 bombing of the Alfred P. Murrah Federal Building in Oklahoma City by individuals with strong beliefs associated with the Christian Identity movement;

- the June 1996 bombing of the Khobar Towers in Saudi Arabia, presumably by Islamic militants; and

- the August 1998 simultaneous bombings of US Embassies in Kenya and Tanzania, blamed on Usama bin Laden.

As a result, we focus considerable attention on the religious fringe and on a host of millennial and apocalyptic groups. At the same time, the scale of terrorist attacks seems to be increasing dramatically, with the events noted here and others suggesting to many that terrorists understand they need an ever-larger 'bang' to get or maintain desired levels of publicity. Consequently, we worry considerably about the potential for terrorist use of chemical, biological, radiological, or nuclear weapons. The Rajneeshis in Oregon, Aum Shinrikyo in Tokyo, and the Chechens in Moscow[6] contributed immensely to these fears.

Academic Literature

The academic literature offered in the past decade has done little to effectively address or test such popular notions. Much like the popular literature, academia has offered visions of worst-case scenarios and horrific 'what-if' considerations. Jessica Stern, in *The Ultimate Terrorists*, for example, opens her consideration of the likelihood of terrorist use of WMD by outlining the potential death and destruction that would be brought about by terrorist use of a simple, homemade nuclear device. With New York City's Empire State Building as the imagined ground zero, Stern notes that such a crude device would likely create a 300ft diameter fireball, destroying the building and leaving in its place a 120ft wide crater. The roughly 20,000 people who work in the building or its immediate environs would be vaporized. Buildings within 600 feet would collapse, as would the area's underground infrastructure, including subway tunnels, killing countless more. In her scenario, such a blast would bring the immediate death of not just those in the immediate area, but of all the individuals up to a quarter of a mile away.

Beyond the range of immediate death, a lethal dose of fallout, measuring a quarter of a mile by nine miles, would kill those affected within two weeks. As far as 18 miles away, there would be enough radiation from the device to cause radiation sickness, with greater incidence of cancer for years hundreds of miles away. According to Stern, the eventual toll in terms of dead, injured, and sickened, could easily reach 100,000 to 200,000 persons.[7] It is not, however, just Stern's vision since such literary devices and scenarios, used to paint a picture of the potential outcome of terrorist use of WMD, have become prevalent in the related literature.[8]

More pervasive, perhaps, in the literature is the emergence of the radical religious individual and group as the greatest single threat, offering the greatest likelihood of WMD use. Most likely stemming from a misreading of David Rapoport's 'Fear and Trembling: Terrorism in Three Religious Traditions',[9] many subsequent authors have assumed or asserted a purely religious-based explanation for this evolution of terrorism. The emerging threat, given this understanding, stems from the expectation that groups act on religious ideology in an effort to address or placate a deity. While Rapoport argued the larger theological framework of the groups shaped perspectives, and consequently actions, of 'sacred' terrorists, others apparently interpreted this to mean that acts of violence are undertaken solely for that ephemeral audience.[10] Subsequent works, some of which build on this misinterpretation, have often taken the religious-imperative-as-explanation as given.[11]

Still others offer alternate interpretations of religion's role ranging from one of several influences to the largest, but not the only explanatory factor.[12] Religion is commonly seen as an important determinant of behavior, whether by shaping or focusing the world-view and cognitive interpretations of adherents, or by directing and dictating all that the adherent does. The power of a religious imperative can be a strong one, driven by the mystery and the presumed divinity of its source or by its close association with a given ethnic identity. As Rapoport argued:

> The transcendent source of holy terror is its most critical distinguishing characteristic; the deity is perceived as being directly involved in the determination of ends and means. ... The modern terrorist [in contrast,] serves political ends to be achieved by human efforts alone, and he, not God, chooses the most appropriate ends and means. It is also true that modern terrorist organizations (especially the most durable and effective ones) are often associated with religious groups, for religion can be a major factor in ethnic identity.[13]

For holy, or religious, terrorists carrying out the will of the deity is paramount. As long as that will, or the tasks perceived as stemming from that will, are seen as divinely ordained, temporal gains and concessions may carry little relevance. Rapoport offers:

Sacred terrorists found their rationale in the past, either in divine instructions transmitted long ago or in interpretations of precedents from founding periods of the parent religion. Their struggles are sanctified with respect to purpose and with respect to means; this is why their violence must have unique characteristics. The very idea of the holy entails contrast with the profane, the normal, or the natural.[14]

Rapoport's assessment suggests a strong purposive content to terrorist acts and motivations. Sacred terror seeks to serve the desires and commands of a deity, or at least to serve the understood desires of the deity. For those who hold themselves to be little more than the instrument used by a deity, those who hold a predestination orientation, the deity remains the principle causal actor and it is in the desires and manipulation of the appropriate tool – man – that the purposive nature is realized. For those taking a more deterministic view, believing perhaps that they can exercise free will within broad deity-defined or -inspired bounds, the purposive component remains largely temporal. And for the hybrid of the two, those who see a role for free will but ultimately with determination resting with some deity, a sense of ability to compel or provoke divine intervention becomes important.[15]

Even more poignantly, the literature on the potential use by terrorists of mass casualty weapons emphasizes the fears and worst-case scenarios which seem to grow from a consideration of religion as a primary causal factor and from the understanding that many such religious groups see their acts as somehow 'doing God's will'. Unlike popular portrayals of the threat, however, academic writings tend to delve further into the decision-making calculus associated with the choice to pursue WMD capabilities. Unfortunately, however, most such assessments are self-limiting in their emphasis on weapons or materiel acquisition or on technical capabilities, or on both. By emphasizing the knowledge needed and the opportunities available for acquisition, many observers elevate practical considerations of the 'how' at the expense of motivational considerations of the 'why'. An acceptance of WMD utility and desirability in the eyes of terrorists is, it seems, often taken as a given in assessments of the potential. Even when the potential for terrorist use of mass casualty weapons is considered very low, the disastrous nature of the outcome, however unlikely it may be, seems to call for a consideration of the means and opportunities available to today's terrorists.[16]

Many of these assessments conclude that sufficient barriers exist which, in one way or another, serve to limit the likelihood of terrorist use of mass casualty weapons. For some, the technical hurdles associated with weapons construction present insurmountable obstacles to all but the most skilled and resource-rich groups. Others see the difficulty in acquiring, holding, and working with raw materials as the principal difficulty acting to limit the likelihood of success. For some, the psychological barrier to the use of mass casualty weapons presents the strongest argument against terrorist WMD use.

Despite the nature of the barriers, whether the limits stem from the ability to successfully gain or build a device, from acquiring necessary skilled personnel or materials, from problems inherent in weaponization itself, or from some other aspect, examinations of the potential for WMD use prevail. Many respected voices, too, have considered the arguments against the likelihood of WMD use and have nevertheless concluded that terrorist use of WMD is, at some point in the future, likely.[17] The debate and disagreement will undoubtedly continue, yet the prevailing treatment in the literature accepts the contention that as long as the possibility exists, the possibility needs to be considered.

Government

Emphasis on the likely evolution of terrorism in the twenty-first century in available government publications largely echoes the prevailing notions and perspectives prevalent in the academic and popular literatures.[18] Given the horrific consequences of terrorist use of mass casualty weapons, coupled with government's role in protecting the nation and its citizens, it seems only natural that government emphasis will rest largely with the greatest possible threat. Nevertheless, current US policy and practice stress the importance of preventive measures and desirability of preventing, preempting, and deterring terrorism.[19] Many of the government's initiatives are, by necessity, hidden from public view if only to protect the sources and methods used in the fight against terrorism.

The public initiatives, on the other hand, place greatest reliance on diplomatic and political cooperation with other states; utilizing all available political, diplomatic, and economic means to dissuade states from sponsoring, supporting, or sheltering terrorists; using all available means to arrest terrorists and bring them to justice, preferably in the United States; or consequence management after an attack.[20]

In one sense, public activities against terrorists rest largely on response and reaction. Bringing terrorists to justice, for example, presupposes the threat or commission of an act of violence. Without the initial terrorist action, be it violent or not, US law offers little opportunity for American action. Even preemptive government activities require cause. Using political, economic, or military capabilities to bear in persuading other states to join the fight against terrorists also presupposes the existence of one or more terrorist groups which have, through words or deeds, indicated an intent to engage in violent activities. Consequence management, quite obviously, encompasses the range of reactive measures to be undertaken after a terrorist action. For each of these areas, the initiative rests largely with the terrorist.

Activities designed to prevent, preempt, or disrupt terrorist activities, by the same token, suggest the need for specific information about the nature of the threat and the intentions of those who might seek to carry that threat to conclusion. Yet there are many groups around the world, and in this country, which have a real grievance against the United States or which work to nurse an imagined grievance. Designing an effective deterrence strategy requires an explicit understanding of that grievance without regard to the grievance's legitimacy. The belief in injustice, oppression, injury, or other insult authored by the United States, its government, its citizens, its businesses or culture drives terrorists to see America or Americans as their opponent.

As the basis for both beliefs and actions, these perceptions hold the key to understanding both terrorist desires and motivations and may, in the same way, offer the key to predicting the extent or scope of future acts. At the same time, an understanding of the perceptions and beliefs of the terrorists offers a window through which we can assess and begin to understand their world-view. This understanding, coupled with an assessment of their observable actions, points toward a greater capacity to predict their actions and their tolerance for counter efforts undertaken by government.

To both grasp the terrorists' perspective and to understand the limits of their tolerance for hardship and opposition demand detailed knowledge of their philosophy or ideology as well as an understanding of the cultural context in which their thoughts and beliefs were born. We must understand their environment as much as we must understand their perspectives if we are to craft a strategy which addresses the limits of their tolerance while also effectively shutting down their ability to evolve and adapt to existing pressures.

But this is, quite possibly, the most difficult task for analysts of terrorism to undertake. Much like understanding the thought processes of mass murderers,[21] understanding the rationale of the terrorist suggests the need to gather exceptionally large amounts of firsthand data which would offer direct insight into the terrorists' thoughts. Even with an effective information gathering system and access by intelligence agencies, the generation of such large volumes of intimate data seems quite daunting. To be effective, intelligence agencies would need unparalleled access to all such groups, on a personal level, along with the ability to predict the emergence of new groups so that infiltration can be accomplished early. And given the number of potentially threatening groups, the clannish nature of many, and existing legal limitations, particularly where American citizens are concerned, one is forced to conclude that such extensive and pervasive infiltration and intelligence gathering is not likely.[22] John Deutch, then Director of Central Intelligence, acknowledged this difficulty in telling a Georgetown University audience that:

> ... we will strive to provide warning of all attacks before they occur, but this is an enormously difficult task. This type of tactical information depends upon access to dedicated terrorist groups who are well financed, skillful, and determined to commit atrocities. Such individuals have learned to keep their planning secret and confined to small cells.[23]

To compensate, the natural tendency is to assess all imagined threats and focus efforts on the most likely and on the most devastating. American policy and practice appear to do just that.[24]

But is this approach the most conducive to developing an effective deterrence strategy? If the success of deterrence can be tied to the applicability of the strategy to the values and desires of the deterrence object, speculation seems prone to missing those aspects of terrorists' motivations and objectives that are most important. Does the prevailing perspective of the terrorist threat, and of its evolutionary potential into the next century, meet the needs of deterrence planners? Given the prevailing perspective's emphasis on worst-case potentials, can we rest assured in the knowledge that counter- and anti-terrorism strategies hold the greatest possible opportunity to effectively prevent, preempt, and defeat terrorists? Or is there an alternative approach which may offer new insights and additional opportunities to attain success or to magnify existing opportunities for success? Shifting our analytic emphasis, it will be argued, offers just such an opportunity to achieve an effective deterrence strategy by addressing the most critical aspects of the terrorists' *raison d'être* than is done at present.

Present Perspectives

A survey of existing popular, academic, and government notions of terrorism yields several broad categories of concern by which the threat can be understood. Foremost among these is the perception of terrorism as evolving from a purposive or instrumental application of violence toward a more ambiguous threat which can, in some instances, retain the purposive and instrumental character, but which can just as easily be undertaken as a simpler expression of hatred and rage.[25]

In the 1960s, 1970s, and into the 1980s, terrorists were seen to act, in large part, in order to achieve some tangible political or social goal. Violence was expected to result in concrete, measurable changes sought by the terrorist. The world, in their eyes, needed to change and they were the instruments for achieving that change.

In recent years, however, the violence has been characterized as more likely to be the result of blind anger and rage, an expression of desperation, or an attempt to affect revenge for real or perceived slights and injustices. No longer were the major acts of terrorism seen as a means to affect a given end. They had become, rather, less predictable and less understandable in the overall context of an irredeemable conflict.[26]

A second, and perhaps more prevalent, theme today is the perspective of the rising threat posed by groups motivated by a religious imperative.[27] Abroad, we see acts of violence authored by groups which claim to be fighting for Islam and against the Zionists, the corrupt and decadent West, or the infidels. We see religiously based violence between Hindus and Buddhists in Sri Lanka and Hindus and Muslims on the Indian subcontinent. We see Aum Shinrikyo experimenting with and using gas purportedly to prepare for the coming apocalypse and hastening the creation of the perfect Buddha-world. We see, in this country, an apparent radicalization of the extreme right, all too frequently coupled with elements of Christian Identity beliefs, resulting in stand-offs in Arkansas, Montana, and Texas as well as the bombing of the Murrah Federal Building in Oklahoma City.

We see, in short, groups motivated by ideas and ideals, by a theology, which appears quite alien to us. We see at times familiar themes, presented and corrupted in ways unimaginable had we not been exposed to it through the medium of violence. We see, as well, suicide bombers both Muslim and Hindu – apparently willing to die in the service of a religious belief. And while that willingness to die for religion is not entirely alien to us, we continue to find it difficult to understand the willingness and enthusiasm with which we see suicide bombers embrace the idea of impending martyrdom. We see, we believe, fellow Americans willing to kill hundreds if not thousands of countrymen in service of a twisted desire to 'purify' the country, to create an idealist white Christian nation. And we do not understand.

We see, in turn, an apparent propensity and greater willingness by these groups to use mass casualty weapons.[28] We hear and read that religious motivations translate into a greater willingness to engage in mass murder and a greater attraction between religiously motivated groups and WMD. We are led to accept the notion, in turn, that cults of any sort have little regard for earthly existence and would be much more willing to hasten the apocalypse through violence. We see the actions of Aum Shinrikyo, of the People's Temple in Jonestown, Guyana, of the Heaven's Gate cultists, of Islamic suicide bombers, of Timothy McVeigh, of those who bombed the World Trade Center, and of Usama bin Laden and, we think there must be something about a religious motive that lends itself toward a greater inherent destructiveness.

Closely associated with our acceptance of the notion that religious groups are more prone to violence is the belief that groups motivated at least in part by their vision of the apocalypse or the new millennium are inherently more dangerous. These groups, we think, are driven by their desire to hasten the apocalypse, to usher forth the end-times and are, consequently, the greatest threat to security. We see the waste and destruction at Jonestown, at the Branch Davidian compound in Waco, and among the Heaven's Gate cult and we wonder whether other, similar, groups might turn their violence outward. We have, in conjunction, observers of such groups warning us that the stressed and the desperate often turn to religion in time of need and that for a significant portion of those people, anger and despair are turned inwards as depression and suicide.

At the same time, another significant segment of that population, we are told, turn their anger and despair outward, resulting in domestic violence, ordinary criminal activity, and, at the extreme, events such as Waco and the Oklahoma City bombing.[29] We see, it seems, a propensity for such groups to assume the mantle of causal agent capable of forcing God's hand and we fear, in turn, that such desires may well lead to greater and more random acts of violence. We wonder, in turn, how we could possibly imagine, much less predict, when a group might turn to religion for solace and when that solace may be turned toward violent aggression.

Taken to the extreme, we also tend to see the greatest threat today from the potential for mass casualty weapons use, particularly by the religiously inspired. We see the tremendous explosion of information available through the Internet, including bomb design and 'recipes' for biological and chemical weapons, and wonder when some group will take advantage of easily available information and access to raw materials. We see the collapse of the Soviet Union and the associated warnings of lost security for mass casualty weapons in Russia and the former Soviet states. We hear repeated warnings over the dangers of proliferation of such weapons, along with the suggestion that dual-use technologies make proliferation control virtually impossible to contain or verify.

We used to accept Brian Jenkins' contention that terrorists want a lot of people watching, not a lot of people dead, and we took comfort in that notion of limited violence. Today, however, we have turned that comforting thought on its head and have come to accept the image of the coldly calculating terrorist intent on killing as many people as absolutely possible for no clear reason. And we see mass casualty weapons as the easiest and most likely avenue by which the terrorist can achieve his goal of utter and wanton destruction. And since the sarin gas attack on the Tokyo subway, we no longer wonder if it will happen but have begun to ask when and where it will happen again.

And finally, we have taken a closer look at our own vulnerabilities, particularly in the wake of the World Trade Center and Murrah Building bombings, and have become more appreciative of the incredible difficulty in hardening all possible terrorist targets. We have begun to feel vulnerable in part because of recent bombings which have shattered our myth of invincibility and unique protection against acts of terror. And we have grown more aware of the sheer scale and complexity of the society we have created and have grown dependent upon.

We have looked at our lives and businesses and have finally realized the extent to which technologically sophisticated opponents, including terrorists, could disrupt and destroy our lives and livelihoods. We look at our dependence on computers and information technology, in particular, and understand the opportunities for terrorists to use basic hacking techniques to disrupt commerce and industry; to insert destructive worms, viruses, and Trojan horses into the very computer systems by which we function and protect ourselves. And we have begun to fear that the computer may be, in part, the next battleground with terrorists.

Questioning the Perspectives

Yet we have to wonder. Are these concerns of the irredeemable conflict, over radical religious groups and their propensity for violence, of apocalypse-inspired motives, of WMD use, and of the specter of cyberterrorism the real threat in the current century? Or are they more a product of our fears and worries? Are they the actual threats we must understand and face in the coming years, or are they perceived threats? Does our vision of the emerging threat match reality, or should we consider readjusting our perceptions so that we might seek a clearer, more balanced understanding of the emergent threat?

It seems, one might argue, that these perceptions have demonstrated the limits of their applicability over the last 20 or 30 years. We have based our counter- and anti-terrorism strategies and tactics on the very ideas and concerns which have given rise to the present general perspectives, yet are no closer to solving the problem of terrorism than we have ever been. It is easy to see how it could be argued that the strategies and tactics employed so far in the fight against terrorism have been successful, for they have forced terrorists to evolve and adapt. The face of terrorism itself has changed, and we would like to think our counter efforts played a large role in bringing about that change. But terrorism remains and, to some, has grown to present a much greater threat than ever before.

We have made little real progress over the past few decades, despite the successes notched against specific groups. Terrorism remains a factor in security planning today, while the terrorists themselves have grown more technically sophisticated and capable. We have, if anything, achieved tactical success, but have lost ground strategically to smaller and more lethal opponents. We have made, in the end, little real and lasting progress across the board in terms of preventing, preempting, and deterring terrorism. Terrorism has changed, but not for the better. We see fewer instances of terrorism in total,[30] but seem to see more terrorist 'spectaculars' with mass casualties than in the past. This observation leads, naturally, to the conclusion of terrorists' greater lethality and greater propensity for mass casualty violence. Coupled with the emergence of vocal religiously-inspired groups, it becomes easy to associate the two and conclude it is the religious motivation which fosters greater levels of violence and a significantly higher threat of violence escalation.

That vision has become quite common today.[31] We see the greater threat from religious groups because we have accepted the notion that they are more prone to violence, are less rational, and are more likely to use mass casualty weapons, particularly if their core beliefs give prominence of place to visions of the apocalypse. Shifting emphasis, however, from our fears toward a more sterile assessment of process may, in the long run, yield greater insights and opportunities for crafting a lastingly effective deterrence strategy.

Terrorism as Process

We can, as others have done in the past, consider terrorism from a system perspective which emphasizes process. In this way, the phenomenon can be seen as a series of inputs, processes, and outputs. Like all other organizations, the terrorist group needs certain inputs in order to function. These would include, but are not limited to, tangible things such as money, arms, safe havens, security, and members, as well as intangibles such as information, appeal, training quality, and rationale or purpose. The inputs, then, would be the sum of all material acquisitions, philosophical foundations, and practices which are needed to plan, coordinate, and undertake an act of rebellion or violence.

With these inputs, the terrorist group would combine and recombine resources, motivations, and information to pull all such elements together for action. Whereas other organizations undertake more benevolent activities, the terrorist group uses an essentially similar resource base for violence. We might suggest, then, that from a systemic process perspective, all organizations and groups, regardless of purpose, practice, legitimacy, or potential for violence share at least the basics of inputs and process. What distinguishes the terrorist group from a nonviolent organization lies in the nature of the output. For the benevolent and peaceful organization, the end result of the application of inputs to satisfy processes generates a service or product which others find useful. For the terrorist, on the other hand, the process of utilizing group inputs becomes the threat or act of violence.

When assessing terrorism, however, analysis most often emphasizes the set of inputs. Critical importance is attached to gathering and exploiting, or understanding, information associated with the terrorists' development and refinement of capabilities. The origin of terrorists' supplies, for example, is considered important for helping isolate and disrupt supply avenues through which the terrorist gains the necessary tools of his or trade trade. The information available to the terrorist, whether generated by the terrorist in person through research and observation, or acquired from an outside source remains important for deterrence planning. It is in this area in which we are best able to anticipate future terrorist actions. Our counter-terrorist and anti-terrorist efforts are, in turn, focused on disrupting the terrorists' ability to gain necessary inputs, or in the case of organic inputs, focused on disrupting the terrorists' ability to fully exploit whatever has been gained.

In emphasizing inputs, assessments of terrorism have long considered the philosophy or ideology which motivates the terrorist as a critical input. Understanding that ideology, we are told repeatedly, is essential for an understanding of what drives the terrorist to adopt the gun and the bomb. Through their actions and their propaganda, terrorists bolster this idea by explicitly linking their ideology to their targets in proclaiming the rationale for their choice of target. The target, they tell us, somehow deserved the violence directed against it; that some act, lack of action, or simple act of association of the target resulted in targeting.

Leftists, then, remind us of their need to confront and attack the oppressive capitalist system which enslaves or exploits the worker.

The radical right, by the same token, feels compelled to tell us they are acting to protect and preserve the sanctity and purity of the state, the ethnic group, or the nobility of some ideal or cause.

The religiously motivated, in turn, tell us that only by seeing and believing as they do will we have hope of salvation; that without seeing the truth as they see it we are doomed to suffer.

The motivating ideology or religious belief is consequently taken by analysts to be the most important driving input and that those sets of beliefs, in large part, determine terrorists' actions, shape their world views, and focus the nature of input and the scope of processes employed. Yet we seem no closer to more fully understanding the way in which these ideological inputs determine terrorists' actions then we were 10 or 20 years ago.

Further, with each 'new' driving ideology which emerges, as religions seems to have done over the last decade, we are forced to begin anew our quest for understanding.

We can, however, turn our analysis around and, rather than emphasizing inputs, focus our attention on the outputs of the systemic process. We can ask what the terrorist is trying to tell us, by both words and deeds, and ask how that message fits with and derives from the terrorists' own ideology or belief system. Moving beyond the surface, however, is necessary for such an examination since consideration of the surface alone limits us to addressing rhetoric alone. We cannot simply ask about the rhetoric, since the rhetoric itself frequently fits into a rather uncomplicated pattern offering little real meaning and little opportunity to determine true intentions and motives.[32] To the extent the terrorists' target and audiences have been considered, we have largely considered each in terms of importance of the target or of the impact of an attack against that target. Alternately, we may find greater value in looking beyond identity of the terrorists' victim or impact of the attack[33] and consider the way in which the target and the means of attack reflect what is going on in the terrorists' minds. Rather than assess target and audience as an end or goal for the terrorists, we can consider each a critical component of the message.

The terrorist seeks to send a message. That itself is not a new or novel idea. Propaganda of the deed and political theater are long-standing ideas associated with the consideration of terrorists' targets and actions. Yet through the years we seem to have looked at terrorist attacks as an end result, sufficient alone for our analysis. The terrorist wants to achieve a goal, affect a change, make demands and receive the object of those demands, or simply lash out in rage and the target, means of attack, and audience identity were seen as manifestations of those wants. The terrorist engages in these acts, we have long argued, through the ultimate act of violence, or in some cases the threat of violence. The act itself, in such a view, becomes culmination of desires, expectations, inputs and processes for which no additional distinctions can be made. Terrorism, simply, has been seen as a linear series of events, with violence as the final output. And that perspective limits us to what we might do to prevent and preempt terror by forcing us to curtail prematurely our own considerations and investigations and focus on disrupting that linear process flow.

We need, however, to be a bit subtler and see terrorism as more of a dialogue or discourse between the terrorist and his audience. We need to look at terrorism as a series of interactions, of message and response, as continuing dialogue which can be shaped, molded, and turned aside through appropriate means at almost any point in the process. Rather than seeing terrorism as something best met head-on, we may want to consider the relationship between terrorist and society as a reciprocal relationship subject to diversion and evolution, one which does not necessarily demand direct confrontation.

How can we do this? By considering the terrorists' message itself, stripped of bias and prejudice, free from emotional reaction, and disassociated from its simplistic rhetorical elements. We should ask what the terrorist, through words and deeds, is really trying to tell us. We need to, and can, dig for the deeper hidden meaning in terrorists' pronouncements and actions. Through this analysis, we can begin to finally appreciate the ways in which terrorists' actions are a call to society, a call which can be responded to in several ways.

Equally important is a need to reassess our own notions of the importance of the terrorists' audience. Again, there is little on the surface new to such a notion, yet a subtle shift in our own consideration may offer tangible benefits which would otherwise go unrealized. We typically see the terrorists' audience in terms or immediate and secondary victims, taking something of a deconstructionist approach in asking ourselves who would be most affected by the terrorists' actions. We can shift this perspective, however, and pose the same question in terms of the terrorists' own perceptions. We can, then, ask who the terrorist thinks he or she is speaking to. Our understanding of the audience is not as important as that of the terrorist, for it is the terrorists' intended audience which should most clearly match their motivations, ideology, and objectives.

We can, in a sense, consider the systemic process of terrorism as if the terrorist has a commodity to sell. And in this case, the commodity is influence. What is the demand for attention, the demand for concession, or the demand for policy change if not a demand for influence over politics? The terrorist most certainly wants to affect some sort of change through purposive actions. Regardless of the nature of the change sought, those demands are the terrorists' effort to establish and exercise a degree of say in the course of events. In this way the terrorist can exert influence without necessarily having to assume primary agency, with all its attendant responsibilities and restraints.

Even when the terrorist does not seek clearly purposive outcomes, when the primary intent is simply to destroy or punish, he or she still seeks influence, although of a more final and deterministic sort. In this case, the ability to destroy or punish is an extreme manifestation of the exercise of influence. It is, in a sense, the terrorists' way of saying that they have the ability to exercise ultimate influence and determine, consequently, the limits to which others may function.

Seeing terrorism in terms of efforts to gain and assert influence allows us to transcend the artificial boundaries we have constructed in our analysis of terrorism. Consideration of influence as the primary driving force of terrorist actions allows us to clear these boundaries by freeing our analysis from the limits imposed by our own ideological considerations, biases, and labels associated with efforts to characterize and distinguish operative ideological motives of terrorists.

All terrorists seek a measure of influence over events, with only the degree and direction of effort varying from group to group and over time. Terrorists of the extreme left and right seek to have a say in the political and institutional aspects of society. The opponent of each may differ, and the expected beneficiary of violent acts may be polar opposites, yet political terrorists of every stripe seek to affect change by persuading or forcing compliance. By the same token, religiously motivated groups, past and present, seek to exert influence with respect to a deity, to act as an agent of manifesting the deity's will or as bridge between the deity and man, or to influence co-religionists or potential converts. The audience may be quite different from that of a secular group, but the religious terrorist still seeks to gain favor or demonstrate loyalty or agency with respect to an assumed audience, either of which being a manifestation of influence.

Both message and intended audience are critical to a better and more nuanced understanding of terrorists and their actions. For example, the Red Army Faction (RAF)[34] sought to liberate the German people from the oppression of the capitalist system so dominated by the United States. To help achieve their goal, the RAF firebombed department stores, kidnapped industrialists and bankers, and shot at captains of industry and representatives of both the German state and of NATO. The primary intended audience of the RAF, as the members of the group saw the struggle, was the German public. It was toward this constituency that the RAF's principal message was directed. 'We are acting to liberate you from oppression', they thought they shouted through words and deeds. Yet the message seemed to fall on deaf ears and had little relevance to the average German citizen, eventually forcing the RAF to acknowledge that their own presumed constituency simply was not listening. The German government, the United States, and NATO were, if anything, secondary audiences of the RAF as the groups desperately tried to generate public support for the struggle.

Similarly, the bombers of the Khobar Towers complex in Saudi Arabia and of the US Embassies in Kenya and Tanzania, whoever they may turn out to be, can be seen as having several core constituencies. Understanding these constituencies, and the messages directed at them, allows us a greater appreciation of the intentions behind the acts. For all three bombings, the primary core constituency appears quite clearly to be the US government. The message was then both a demand to the US to cease its 'occupation' of

Saudi lands and a warning that US targets, however distant from the Middle East, could be effectively and efficiently targeted.

The American public, additionally, was a secondary audience for the bombers who sought to reinforce the demands and warnings to the government with the American people while also suggesting that the American people demand its government 'bring our boys home'. Finally, the bombers also sought to communicate with the Islamic world emphasizing the message that the attacks were undertaken to protect Muslim lands, values, and culture from the occupation and corruption of the decadent West.

A New Set of Emerging Threats?

Considering terrorism an effort to gain and assert influence, albeit a violent effort, leads naturally to a reconsideration of the nature of emerging terrorist threats. Holding the message and the terrorists' expected and perceived audiences to be of greater importance than other factors, we begin to shift understanding of emergent threats away from a narrow ideologically-based view affected by prejudice, bias, and ignorance.[35] In the case of religiously motivated groups, in particular, our lack of understanding of the theological underpinnings or our misinterpretation of those beliefs has led to an almost automatic consideration of religious groups as increasingly threatening.[36] We have assumed, consequently, that religious motivation necessarily means greater tolerance for mass casualties and a greater threat potential. Yet the evidence, as Rapoport (1999) eloquently argues, has not borne that assumption out. Shifting our own perspective towards the effort to gain and exercise influence, on the other hand, offers a more neutral consideration of the threat by incorporating the terrorists' own rationale. What results is, arguably, a more realistic assessment of the emerging threat.

We face a greater threat in the coming years from, first, non-adaptive groups. The Palestine Liberation Organization (PLO) has evolved over the years, striving amidst an ever- changing environment to maintain message relevance among its core constituency. As the perception of a relatively invincible Israeli state began to crumble under the pressure of Hamas and Hizballah activities in Lebanon and of the *intifada* in the West Bank and Gaza Strip, the sense began to emerge that concessions could be won from the Israeli government. Coupled with a weariness over the Israelis' ability to impose and maintain severe economic sanctions on Palestinians under its control, the PLO came to understand that peaceful means would likely offer greater opportunities to achieve influence and results than would continued terrorist attacks, while also offering an opportunity to maintain a constructive dialogue with the Palestinian people.

The RAF, on the other hand, failed to adapt its message to meet the interests, expectations, and values of the German people they claimed to represent, sealing in turn their own irrelevance. By the same token, the Iranian Mujahedin-e Khalq aliened its core constituency, the Iranian people, by actively siding with Iraq in the 1980s.[37]

Aum Shinrikyo,[38] on the other hand, exhibited no desire to adapt their message to the Japanese government or Japanese people, believing that they knew the truth and all who wanted salvation had to accept Aum's version of that truth. Those who did not accept that truth, and Shoko Asahara's clarity of vision, would, by Aum's philosophy, perish accordingly. Unlike the Mujahedin and RAF, however, Aum chose not to adapt, based on its absolute certainty that Asahara alone knew truth. Aum's subsequent actions provided a clear and unambiguous indicator that the group's concern for public opinion was minimal at best. Unique, perhaps, among terrorist groups, Aum Shinrikyo cared little for popular support, preferring to win converts among those who could progress along the true path of enlightenment and ignoring all others.

Rather than failing to adapt, Aum chose not to, highlighting the type of group characterized here as non-adaptive. It is a purposive non-adaptation which suggests threat, since it is just such a group which offers little if any importance to the desires, expectations, and values of larger society. Social mores are not simply misjudged, misinterpreted, and misapplied, as was the case with the RAF and Mujahedin, but rejected outright. Such groups exhibit clear and uncompromising disdain for the normal restraints afforded by society, preferring to destroy and reconstruct all social institutions rather than working within the framework of social structures to affect change.

It is perhaps comforting to note that so far only one group – Aum Shinrikyo – appears to have made the conscious choice of rejecting societal frameworks while simultaneously directing aggression outward.[39] Fully committed groups forced into adopting desperate measures may also conclude that social structures and norms no longer provide the opportunity to seek satisfaction of desires, resulting in a rejection of once-accepted standards of and limits to behavior. The Chechen rebels, perhaps, might offer an example of how this possibility might come to pass.

Second, greater threats may emerge from *ad hoc* groups. Like Usama bin Laden's organization, such structures are more akin to loose networks of associations than to organizations. Largely lacking hierarchical structures, networks of terrorists will coalesce, act, then dissolve in response to transient concerns and goals. *Ad hoc* groups, by nature, would be quite fluid, offering little opportunity for analysts and deterrence planners to fully appreciate existing vulnerabilities in the terrorists' network. With fewer opportunities to find and exploit vulnerabilities, crafting an effective and efficient deterrence strategy will be forced to fall back on use of frameworks and templates from past counter- and anti-terrorist planning. And with reliance on previous efforts comes a lessened ability to tailor reactions and preemptive measures to the specifics of the threat. Newly crafted associations of terrorists, established for limited purposes and for a limited time, do not offer issue salience or continuity to the counterterrorism community. Consequently, *ad hoc* groupings like Usama bin Laden's offer a greater threat than might otherwise be the case given a hierarchical structure, some semblance of organizational permanence, and similar capabilities.

A third major emergent threat stems from the explosive growth of communications capabilities and information leveraging. The growth and affordability of computers, coupled with the inherent anarchy of the Internet, offers the terrorist a myriad of opportunities to put communications, computer, and information technologies to work on his or her group's behalf. To date, however, much of the concern has revolved around the potential for terrorist use of computer technologies to disrupt and destroy critical computer-dependent infrastructures. Terrorists might, we are told, use computers to take down an air traffic control system, causing any number of commercial aircraft to crash or collide. Terrorists could, we fear, significantly imperil the American economy by accessing and disrupting Wall Street's ability to maintain market vitality and operations.

We should ask ourselves, however, what benefit terrorists would derive from such acts and, even more importantly, how the terrorists would convince us that they, in fact, were responsible for the acts they claim credit for. How do we know, for example, that a computer system intrusion is not the work of a teenaged hacker unaffiliated with any group? And given the sophistication of the terrorists' adversaries, should we not expect the terrorist to at least consider the potential which exists by which his adversaries can harness the computer and communications available to shut down the terrorists' access?

Rather than envisioning a cyberterrorist threat built along the lines of offensive operations, the greater threat may stem from terrorists using available technologies in a more accepted manner. We should recall that terrorists seek, first and foremost, influence. In the past, to gain influence the terrorist relied on the mass media or on proximity to an intended audience. Without the advent of global communications, terrorists' audiences were largely limited to the people in the immediate vicinity of their area of operations. Television opened the door to a global reach, offering terrorists the opportunity to reach a much wider audience in a timely manner. Escalation of violence, and the advent of terrorist 'spectaculars' consequently grabbed our attention. But as we have become somewhat jaded and immune to daily replays of the latest terrorist event, and as the limits of our tolerance for spectaculars is demonstrated by our reactions to recent attacks, technologically savvy terrorists may well consider technological evolution as an opportunity more than as a weapon. Whereas the terrorist of the past had limited options for spreading his message and generating sympathy for his cause, the terrorist of today and the future can reach a worldwide audience with a few clicks of a mouse. How many people outside of Mexico would have known of the struggle in Chiapas state were it not for the Internet? How little public sympathy would have resulted? Internet sites operated by or on behalf of terrorist groups effectively seize the power of the Internet in offering stunning graphics, colorful displays, and hard-hitting messages designed to win support – in ways largely safe from sanction by their opponents. Besides offering a vehicle for generating public awareness and sympathy, the Internet also offers terrorists a way of identifying and recruiting members, supporters, and sympathizers from among a much larger audience than ever before. The threat, it seems, in the coming years lies in this area – the opportunity to recruit from among a global constituency and to address and harness the sympathetic expressions of that sympathy[40] – rather than in the use of computer and communications technology offensively.

What does this mean for our efforts to counter and deter terrorism? In planning to meet the coming challenges, we need to think more like the terrorists, asking ourselves why they would undertake a certain set of actions. We need to ask who it is the terrorist thinks he or she is addressing and to ask what the terrorist is trying to say. We need to delve more deeply into the dynamics of that dialogue between terrorist and opponent to understand more fully the motives and expectations of the terrorist. In doing so, we might then be able to tease out an understanding of what matters most to each organization, to understand where that organization is vulnerable, and to understand how best to deflect the terrorists' ability to effectively gain and maintain relevance with their core constituency. Terrorism can be disrupted at any number of points. Finding and then exploiting those vulnerability points are the keys to developing and implementing an effective deterrence strategy. That strategy, for maximum effectiveness, needs to be flexible and focused.

Focused on the desires, expectations, grievances, and capabilities of the terrorists themselves, and focused on the desires, expectations, hopes, and tolerances of the larger public. Terrorism is a contest of influence more so than it is a contest for control or power. The most effective deterrence strategy in the twenty-first century will approach the challenge as such.

NOTES

1. US President, *A National Security Strategy for a New Century* (Washington DC: The White House Oct. 1998).
2. Ibid. p.18.
3. Recent and well known examples of such portrayals include Tom Clancy's *The Sum of All Fears* (NY: Putnam 1991); Richard Preston's *The Cobra Event* (NY: Random House 1997); and movies such as 'True Lies', 'Arlington Road', and 'The Peacemaker'.
4. Indicative of this literature are the recent publications released by the US General Accounting Office. Recent titles include: *Combating Terrorism: Federal Agencies' Efforts to Implement National Policy and Strategy* (GAO/NSIAD-97-254, Sept. 1997); *Combating Terrorism: Observations on the Nunn-Lugar-Domenici Domestic Preparedness Program* (GAO/T-NSIAD-99-16, Oct. 1998); *Combating Terrorism: Opportunities to Improve Domestic Preparedness Focus and Efficiency* (GAO/NSIAD-99-3, Nov. 1998); *Combating Terrorism: Issues to be Resolved to Improve Counterterrorism Operations* (GAO/NSIAD-99-135, May 1999); *Combating Terrorism: Analysis of Federal Counterterrorist Exercises*, GAO/NSIAD-99-157BR, June 1999); *Combating Terrorism: Analysis of Potential Emergency Response Equipment and Sustainment Costs* (GAO/NSIAD-99-151, June 1999); and *Combating Terrorism: Observations on Growth in Federal Programs* (GAO/T-NSIAD-99-181, June 1999).
5. For examples of how this portrayal has affected our perceptions and the questions we ask about the phenomenon, see Clarence J. Bouchat, 'Suicide Bombers: Business as Usual', *Studies in Conflict and Terrorism* 19 (1996) pp.329–37; and David G. Kibble, 'The Threat of Militant Islam: A Fundamental Reappraisal', pp.353–64. Both Bouchat and Kibble argue the perspective and perception of threat are not congruent with reality.
6. Members of the Rajneesh religious commune sickened a large number of people in the vicinity of Antelope, Oregon, in the late 1970s by spreading botulism toxin in local salad bars, reportedly to lower voter turnout in order to secure election to one or more commune members. Aum Shinrikyo has been the author of several well-publicized chemical and biological attacks or attempts. Chechen militants have claimed credit for leaving cesium 137 in a central Moscow park in 1996 in retaliation for Russian military actions in Chechnya. There have been, additionally, some 10,000 anthrax scares in this country since the Tokyo sarin gas attack.
7. Jessica Stern, *The Ultimate Terrorists* (Cambridge, MA; Harvard UP 1999) pp.1–5.
8. See also Walter Laqueur, *The New Terrorism: Fanaticism and the Arms of Mass Destruction* (NY: Oxford UP 1999); Ian Lesser *et al.*, *Countering the New Terrorism* (Santa Monica, CA: RAND 1999); Joseph W. Foxell Jr, 'The Debate on the Potential for Mass-Casualty Terrorism: The Challenge to US Security', *Terrorism and Political Violence* 11/1 (Spring 1999) pp.94–109; Bruce Hoffman, 'Holy Terror: The Implications of Terrorism Motivated by a Religious Imperative', *Studies in Conflict and Terrorism* 18 (1995) pp.271–84, to list but a few. The literature suggesting such scenarios are more the result of fear are relatively few and far between. Notable examples of these are David C. Rapoport, 'Terrorism and Weapons of the Apocalypse', *National Security Studies Quarterly* 5 (1999) pp.49–67; and Ehud Sprinzak, 'The Great Superterrorism Scare', *Foreign Policy* (1998), pp.110–24.
9. David C. Rapoport, 'Fear and Trembling: Terrorism in Three Religious Traditions', *American Political Science Review* 78 (1984) pp.658–77. Rapoport, himself, suggests this may indeed be an unintended consequence of his earlier work. See Rapoport (note 8), footnote 10. I am grateful to Prof. Rapoport for providing not only a prepublication copy of his work, but also an additional explanation of his reasoning.
10. See, for example, Hoffman (note 8) and idem, *Inside Terrorism* (London, UK: Victor Gollancz 1998).
11. Foxell (note 8) for example, writes on p.97,

    A new wave of terrorists, spearheaded by religious fanatics, ethnic-cleansing terror movements, mind-control and millennial cults, 'morality terrorists', and 'for-profit' extortionists has emerged. This coterie reads as a roster of the most likely actors to break terrorism's tacit barrier against using weapons of mass destruction as their idiosyncratic, self-encapsulated world views each qualify a climate in which the world's judgment is unimportant.

12. Examples of this variety could include Lesser (note 8); Roger Medd and Frank Goldstein, 'International Terrorism on the Eve of a New Millennium', *Studies in Conflict and Terrorism* 20 (1997) pp.281–316; Samuel Peleg, 'They Shoot Prime Ministers Too, Don't They? Religious Violence in Israel: Premises, Dynamics, and Prospects', *Studies in Conflict and Terrorism* 20 (1997) pp.227–47; Adam L. Silverman, 'It's the End of the World as We Know It: Millennialism, Political Violence, and Terrorism at the End of the Second Millennium', poster presentation at the 1999 Annual Meeting of the American Political Science Association, Atlanta, Georgia, 2–6 September 1999; Federal Bureau of Investigation, 'Project Megiddo Report', URL http://www.fbi.gov/library/megiddo/publicmegiddo.pdf, 1999, accessed 28 Nov. 1999; Stern (note 7); and various works by Michael Barkun, such as Barkun, 'Conspiracy Theories as Stigmatized Knowledge: The Basis for a New Age Racism?' in Jeffrey Kaplan and Tore Bjørgo (eds.), *Nation and Race: The Developing Euro-American Racist Subculture* (Boston, MA: Northeastern UP 1998) pp.58–72; and Barkun, 'Understanding Millennialism', *Terror and Political Violence* 7/3 (Autumn 1995) pp.1–9.

13. Rapoport (note 9) p.674.

14. Ibid.

15. Ibid. also notes that for the holy terrorist with apocalyptic visions, the '… ultimate concern was to create *the* catastrophe that would compel God to redeem the righteous remnant…' [italics in the original].

16. See, for example, Gavin Cameron, 'The Likelihood of Nuclear Terrorism', *The Journal of Conflict Studies* 18 (1998) pp.5–28, who writes '… why would one use such a weapon [a nuclear device], since acquiring fissile material would involve so much more effort than conventional terrorism? Part of the answer must lie in its publicity value, and the fear it is capable of engendering.' (p.18). Foxell (note 8) provides a clear example of the emphasis on worst-case scenarios and on focused consideration of access and capability involving use of WMD. Others, such as Hoffman (note 8), acknowledge the importance of addressing motivational issues, yet seem to readily fall back on the more familiar topics of capability and access.

17. It should be noted here that some authors acknowledge a likelihood, albeit a slight one, while others have indicated a belief that it will happen with the only real question being when it will. Bruce Hoffman, James Campbell, Gavin Cameron, and Roger Medd and Frank Goldstein are examples of the former, while Yonah Alexander exemplifies the latter.

18. See, for example, CIA Director John M. Deutch, speech presented at the Conference on Nuclear, Biological, Chemical Weapons Proliferation and Terrorism, 23 May 1996. URL http://www.cia.gov/cia/ public_affairs/speeches/archives/1996/dci_speech_052396.html, accessed 31 Jan. 2000.

19. *National Security Strategy* (note 1) p.14. For a handy summary of the Clinton administration's positions and efforts, see also Office of the Press Secretary, 'Factsheet–Counter-Terrorism: The White House's Position on Terrorism', 1999, URL_http:// nsi.org/ Library/Terrorism/policy.html, accessed 31 Jan. 2000.

20. Deputy Chief, DCI Counterterrorism Center, 'International Terrorism: Challenge and Response', speech presented at a meeting of the World Affairs Council, Naples, Florida, 16 Nov. 1998. URL http://www.cia.gov/cia/di/speeches/intlterr.html, accessed 31 Jan. 2000.

21. For an exceptionally readable account of both the scientific basis for criminal 'profiling' and of the practice of using profiles to solve criminal cases, see John Douglas and Mark Olshaker, *Mindhunter: Inside the FBI's Elite Serial Crime Unit* (NY: Scribner's 1998).

22. Spreading intelligence resources thin, and making the hard choices associated with decisions on where to focus those scarce intelligence resources, was aptly highlighted by Special Assistant to the Director of Central Intelligence for Nonproliferation John A. Lauder in March and April 1999. See Lauder, 'Statement by Special Assistant to the DCI for Nonproliferation John A. Lauder on the Worldwide Biological Warfare Threat to the House Permanent Select Committee on Intelligence as Prepared for Delivery on 3 March 1999'. URL http://www.cia.gov/cia/public_affairs/speeches/lauder_speech_ 030399.html, accessed 31 Jan. 2000, and Lauder, 'Unclassified Statement for the Record on the Worldwide WMD

Threat to the Commission to Access the Proliferation of Weapons of Mass Destruction as Prepared for Delivery on 29 April 1999', URL http://www.cia.gov/cia/public_affairs/ speeches/lauder_speech_042999.html, accessed 31 Jan. 2000. While Lauder was speaking specifically of intelligence gathering against biological warfare threats and on the most important 10 of over 50 states that are a proliferation concern, the same certainly applies to non-state actors like terrorists, which, by nature, are even more difficult targets for information gathering. Lauder also notes the connection to terrorism in citing Usama bin Laden's stated desire to acquire WMD capabilities. He notes, further, the great difficulty the intelligence community faces in gathering and then analyzing the tremendous amount of information already available.

23. John Deutch, 'Fighting Foreign Terrorism', speech presented at Georgetown University, 5 Sept. 1996. URL http://www.cia.gov/cia/public_affairs/speeches/archives/1996/dci_speech _090596.html, accessed 31 Jan. 2000.

24. See, for example, the GAO reports and testimony cited in note 4. Also see Rapoport (note 8), pp.50–1; and Martha Crenshaw, presentation at the 1999 scientific meeting of the International Society of Political Psychology in the Netherlands, have argued that the threat and perception of threat, particularly of terrorist use of mass casualty weapons, has created a series of actions and policies driven, perhaps, more by the competition for resources than a realistic assessment of the threat. By the same token, Smith and Thomas have argued that as the perception of threat shifted from international terrorism to domestic terrorism, government perception shifted away from the problem of strategic national security issues toward a domestic law enforcement issue perspective, with an attendant shift from response strategy to response tactics. See James M. Smith and William C. Thomas, 'The Real Threat from Oklahoma City: Tactical and Strategic Responses to Terrorism', *Journal of Conflict Studies* 18 (1998) pp.119–38.

25. See, for example, Cameron (note 16) p.20; Medd and Goldstein (note 12) p.282; Deputy Chief CTC (note 20); and Senior Analytic Manager, DCI Counterterrorism Center, 'The International Terrorist Threat to US Interests', speech presented at the World Affairs Council, San Antonio, Texas, 7 Oct. 1996. URL http://www.cia.gov/cia/di/speeches/428141198.html, accessed 31 Jan. 2000. The latter two emphasize the diverse nature of terrorism while stressing a belief that the greatest single threat today stems from those motivated by a religious belief.

26. See, for example, C.J.M. Drake, 'The Role of Ideology in Terrorists' Target Selection', *Terrorism and Political Violence* 10/2 (Summer 1998) pp.53–85; C.J.M. Drake, *Terrorists' Target Selection* (London, UK: Macmillan Press 1998); and Henry W. Prunckun Jr and Philip B. Mohr, 'Military Deterrence of International Terrorism: An Evaluation of Operation El Dorado Canyon', *Studies in Conflict and Terrorism* 20 (1997) pp.267–80. While each of these works emphasize more specific aspects of terrorism and counters to terrorism, each rests on a view of terrorism as an intractable conflict which can, perhaps, be understood and managed, but probably not solved given the motivations of terrorists today. Other works rest on the same theme and these are offered simply as easily accessible examples.

27. Examples include Hoffman (note 8); Senior Analytic Manager, CTC (note 25); Medd and Goldstein (note 12); Cameron (note 16); Deputy Chief, CTC (note 20); Jonathan Bor, 'Spreading the Word About Bioterrorism', *The Baltimore Sun*, 27 Dec. 1999, edition, sec. 1A+; FBI, 1999; Foxell (note 8); Hoffman (note 10); Laqueur (note 8); Lesser (note 8); and Stern, (note 7).

28. Such a portrayal is all too common in the literature today, offering countless examples. It is, consequently, much easier to note the exceptions. Principal among the exceptions is Rapoport (note 8), who argues, on p.49, that 'The historical record indicates secular groups have sought to use such [mass casualty] weapons more often than religious groups.'

29. This is the overriding theme of authors such as Joel Dyer, *Harvest of Rage: Why Oklahoma City is Only the Beginning* (Boulder, CO: Westview Press 1998).

30. While there are several authors who discuss this trend, a good summary can be found in Walt Enders and Todd Sandler, 'Transnational Terrorism in the Post-Cold War Era', *International Studies Quarterly* 43 (1999) pp.145–67.

31. Rapoport (note 8), notes that he may be the source of that perspective, particularly since

many who offer it cite his article 'Fear and Trembling' (note 9), or cite another author who, in turn, cites–and misinterprets–Rapoport's earlier work. Most interpretations of Rapoport's earlier work take religion as the basis for the evolution of terror, while Rapoport's contention was actually that the traditions and evolution of three great religions gave rise to three separate and distinct ways of violence (and terror) that are addressed in the religious context.

32. See, for example, Richard W. Leeman, *The Rhetoric of Terrorism and Counterterrorism* (NY: Greenwood Press 1991). Leeman demonstrates how terrorist rhetoric and counterterrorist rhetoric often mirror each other in words and content and shows how each is generally geared more toward persuading the general public rather than being designed to effectively communicate beliefs or demands.

33. Drake (note 26) offers an in-depth analysis linking terrorists' target selection with motivations and objectives. This is one of the better examples of an effort to move beyond an input-focused assessment.

34. Excellent narratives on the evolution and operations of the RAF and similar German groups include Michael 'Bommi' Baumann, *Terror or Love? Bommi Baumann's Own Story of His Life as a West German Urban Guerrilla* (NY: Grove Press 1997); and Jillian Becker, *Hitler's Children: The Story of the Baader-Meinhof Terrorist Gang* (Philadelphia, PA: Lippincott 1997).

35. Ignorance here is intended to mean nothing more than the lack of understanding or awareness.

36. This is certainly a contentious issue. All too often, however, an incomplete understanding of the appropriate religious beliefs leads to a misinterpretation of motives, methods, and objectives as Rapoport (note 8), points out. Poor or incomplete Western understanding of Islam, for example, has lead to a fairly common stereotype of the fundamentalist Muslim undertaking *jihad*, or holy war, against all things Western. Unfortunately, however, that stereotype plays on an incomplete understanding of *jihad* and a failure to appreciate the distinction Islam makes between greater *jihad* and lesser *jihad*. Two who do incorporate a more in-depth understanding of Islam and who argue against the more common misperception of Islam's potential as a threat are Kibble (note 5), and Bouchat (note 5).

37. US Department of State, *People's Mojahedin of Iran*, report produced in accordance with P.L. 103-236, section 523 (Washington, DC: Dept. of State 1994).

38. One of the best accounts of Aum Shinrikyo's beliefs, evolution, and activities is Manabu Watanabe, 'Religion and Violence in Japan Today: A Chronological and Doctrinal Analysis of Aum Shinrikyo', *Terrorism and Political Violence* 10/4 (Winter 1998) pp.80–100.

39. Until Aum, other groups which rejected social structures and norms outright turned their aggression inward in an effort to either punish group members for impurities or perceived failings or to punish society by affecting absolute and total withdrawal. This behavior appears characteristic of many cults and, until Aum, the best examples included the People's Temple in Jonestown, Guyana, the Branch Davidians in Waco, Texas, and the Heaven's Gate and Solar Temple cults.

40. The ease and effectiveness of this kind of use can be seen in the success of the movement to ban landmines, much of which was generated at a grassroots level through the use of the Internet and communications technologies. Similarly, the summoning and organization of protests in Seattle, Washington, and then in Washington DC, during World Trade Organization talks was largely accomplished via the Internet.

Countering Traumatic Attacks

RICHARD DANZIG

For millennia, offensive warfare has aimed to destroy, degrade, or capture an opponent's troops weapons, property, and territory. Since the European invention of gunpowder in the fourteenth century, the main means of doing this has been by explosive weaponry: bullets, bombs, mines, and missiles. Another risk to American security over the next decades is that both this aim and these means may change. The aim will not be to destroy American military power (that is too difficult), but rather to sap the will to use it. The means will be nonexplosive warfare, conducted with Newly Emergent Warfare (NEW) weapons. The manifestation of these changes will be 'traumatic attacks'.

How do NEW weapons differ from their predecessors? What special aims of traumatic attacks are amplified when these weapons are used? What kinds of investments would diminish risks from these weapons and these types of attacks? This analysis describes three broad changes, going well beyond our traditional reliance on deterrence, that are likely to be necessary if we are to maintain our security in the twenty-first century.

In the late twentieth century, traumatic attacks have predominantly employed explosive munitions placed in or near buses, cars, airplanes, and buildings. Accordingly, we now focus on explosives when we attempt to protect the security of airports, military bases, government buildings, and other key facilities and means of transport at home and abroad. At the same time, we are making well-warranted efforts to reduce and control the world stockpile of nuclear weapons.

The dangers of the future, against which we are underprotected, arise from NEW weapons, predominantly biological and information warfare, secondarily from chemical or radioactive materials. Attacks of this kind are less familiar but have grave potential for causing mass disruption, panic, and (in the case of biological weaponry) deaths that could be counted in the hundreds of thousands.

An understanding of the most novel activities, biological and information warfare, will illuminate the character of these weapons.[1] Biological attack is the dissemination of bacteria, viruses, or toxins to cause debilitating or fatal illness through breathing, drinking, or absorption. Weapons of this kind are extraordinarily potent. It has been calculated that a millionth of a gram of anthrax will first sicken and then, within a week, kill anyone who inhales it; taking account of dissipation and delivery over a metropolitan area, a kilogram has the potential to kill a million people.[2] If an infectious agent like plague or smallpox is used, a chain reaction can be induced, and the effects of an incident may be unbounded. Beyond its ability to kill, a biological attack can be highly disruptive. Sickness induces panic and psychosomatic effects. Large numbers of people in panic, flight, and illness can quickly overwhelm our regular systems of care, transportation, and communication.

It is striking how analogous information attacks are to their biological counterparts. We even use similar terminology when we describe a computer 'virus'. A single computer virus, like its biological equivalent, can have widespread and proliferating effects. Whether embedded in software in advance or disseminated near the time of use, a computer virus can destroy or distort data in the information and communication systems upon which military and civilian life depends. The gravity of the Year 2000 problem – a 'natural occurrence' that corresponds to information attack, as natural outbreaks of disease do to biological warfare – highlights our dependence upon, and yet the vulnerability of, information and communication systems.

Biological and information attacks share more than a dozen characteristics that can make future security problems very different from today's. These attacks will not depend on, or be defeated by, mass, either of armies or of physical barricades. They do not require large, visible methods of production. Potent biological weapons can be made in a room and held in a vat. The forces of cyberspace can be marshaled on a desk and stored on a disk. The skills and assets required to wage this kind of war are very like those associated with legitimate civilian activities in the pharmaceutical and computer industries and are rather readily and inexpensively obtained. Once prepared, these weapons will not require missiles, shells, or other very visible, technically demanding, or expensive methods of delivery.

A single computer can launch an information attack. An ordinary crop sprayer can generate a fatal anthrax cloud over 80 miles long. A single leased airplane dispersing a biological agent can kill more people than died in any month of World War II. The effects of these attacks can occur for substantial periods after delivery, and consequences must be measured by the uncertainty, panic and physical effects they will cause.

Distinguishing among crime, terrorism, natural occurrences, and war become difficult when NEW weapons are used. Because large financial resources, massing power, and delivery systems are not required, it is not necessary to be a major nation to be able to conduct this type of warfare. Though subject to use by a major competitor, second- or third-tier states, subnational groups, or even individuals may present threats from biological and information warfare. A large industrial base is not required to develop or deploy NEW weapons, because they are postindustrial weapons; in the postindustrial era, the power to wage war is no longer monopolized by nation-states.

Furthermore, the characteristics of low visibility, delay, and natural occurrence can be exploited to leave uncertainty as to whether a military attack occurred and, if it did, who conducted it. This makes retaliation difficult. Because deterrence depends on a credible ability and will to retaliate, deterrence will not be as effective in suppressing traumatic attacks as it is in discouraging other forms of warfare.

These are fast-growing technologies. While explosive weapons and their delivery systems take decades to evolve and produce, NEW weapons multiply in variety and potency with a speed that characterizes the biotechnology and software industries from which they stem. Defenses typically cannot keep pace with offenses that are so easily varied and proliferated.

Taken together, more than a dozen attributes differentiate these weapons. They cannot be countered by the usual methods. Worse still, we are handicapped in recognizing changes needed to counter these weapons. The military establishment is not attuned to these issues. The familiar weapons are explosive weapons. The familiar battles are the clash of armies, navies and air forces. Familiar battlefields are the places where militaries grapple with their opposite numbers. The traditional business of warfare is explosive weaponry, not disease (the province of doctors) or information (a support function).

Further, we do not have well-developed offensive programs that might inform and stimulate our defensive efforts. Since 1969, we have refrained from any offensive program involving biological weapons. The decision to refrain from an offensive program, though appropriate, is like the amputation of an arm; the military is struggling to grasp a load with one hand when it is used to using two. The offensive possibilities of information warfare are more readily understood, but, in part because of our own vulnerabilities, we are inhibited about practicing and openly debating the offensive aspects of information 'traumatic attack'. Consequently, in this area also, our ability to grasp the risk (and to counter it) is weak.

For their part, civilian authorities are not used to looking upon their domains as battlefields. The Federal Bureau of Investigation (FBI) is concerned with developing criminal cases; the Centers for Disease Control, the Public Health Service, and local power companies are focused on natural events, not defense against attacks. Our military and civilian agencies are not commonly or easily coordinated. We are, in short, ill positioned for coping with NEW weapons and most especially so if these weapons are used in 'traumatic attacks' against our civilian populations.

NEW weapons can be employed in traditional military settings or to undermine reinforcement and to mass in preparation for conventional warfare. But both biological and information warfare is more potent in less conventional circumstances: it can be used to gain bargaining leverage by threatening civilian populations and to induce a distracting and dispiriting panic in those populations. However vulnerable troops and military information systems may be, civilians are vastly more so. While military forces enjoy a modicum of protective clothing, encrypted systems, and other barriers to biological and information attack, civilian populations are highly vulnerable. Troops are trained and disciplined for combat; civilians, especially American civilians, are not prepared.

Warfare aimed at civilian populations would not be assessed by body counts or territory occupied, but by how the minds of the American public and that of allied populations were affected. Alvin and Heidi Toffler have pointed out that ways of making war reflect ways of making wealth.[3] In an agricultural age, battles were fought with agricultural instruments (such as horses and swords), the unit of value was land, and victory was achieved by occupation of territory. Industrial-era wars are fought with the products of industry (e.g., engines and explosives), and victory is achieved by destruction. In the information age, information and telecommunications are likely to be principal weapons, and molding perceptions may constitute victory.[4]

We have not yet reached the point where perceptions can be molded without events. Traumatic attacks are the thin end of the wedge by which public opinion can be leveraged, the hook on which perceptions can be hung. The hallmark of these attacks is that they are valued not for their physical effects but for their psychological consequences. It was not the occupation of territory or the disablement of the American military machine that determined the value of the Tet Offensive in Viet Nam, the bunker bomb in Lebanon in 1983, or the massacre of soldiers before Cable News Network cameras in Somalia in 1993. Of course, traumas can have the opposite effect and instead multiply national determination; the Alamo, the battleship *Maine* sinking, and Pearl Harbor became rallying cries precisely *because* of the injury they inflicted. However, these were not designed to be traumatic attacks. In retrospect, we can see that the attackers did not understand the psychological consequences of achieving their material goals. These experiences warn the designers of traumatic attacks that they are working with a most potent power that may backfire or get out of control in unexpected ways. The handling of the consequences of events may be more important than controlling the events themselves.

A first and right instinct is to protect ourselves against the NEW weapons. Though we cannot be totally successful in these efforts, we can do a great deal. To defend against biological attack, we can secure large benefits from rapid development and deployment of detector technology; investment in antibiotic and vaccine research; stockpiling of medicines and vaccines; inoculation; refinement and acquisition of simple form-fitted masks to prevent infection by inhalation; improved intelligence, enhanced training; and development of doctrine about how to preempt and, when necessary, respond to a biological attack.

Our defense against information warfare similarly demands more innovative preparation. Our aim should be to prevent intrusions and alterations of data that can misdirect missiles, airplanes, ships, and spare parts and distort financial, utility, telecommunication, and other systems upon which we depend. A deeper perception of these vulnerabilities should lead to greater investments in intelligence and in research and product development for computer and communications security. We should reflect the state of our defenses against these vulnerabilities in our readiness systems, include it in the training of officers, and exercise information protection along with our other defensive skills.

Our efforts to defend against traumatic attacks, however, demand more than the application of these traditional approaches to the new areas of biological and information warfare. Above all, they demand challenging shifts in our conceptual framework. In addition to defense, we need to tailor strategies of dissuasion, deterrence, disruption, and consequence management to the challenges of NEW weapons.

To reduce the risk of a military competition, a theory of dissuasion needs to take its place alongside theories of deterrence. Dissuasion seeks to avert the development of a major military competitor; deterrence seeks to limit the actions of an established competitor. NEW should emphasize the benefits of pursuing dissuasive strategies even with nations that are not likely to be major competitors. Because NEW weapons can be used or proliferated by second- and third-tier states – even, for example, by a poverty-stricken North Korea or an isolated Iran – there is a security reason for trying to tie these states into the community of nations. To counter weapons of mass disruption, it is desirable to bring countries that may be opposed to us to a point where they have a stake in maintaining the world system and thus in avoiding disruption.

Working from a position of military and economic superiority, we can afford, and in our own interests should pursue, openhanded, cooperative strategies that avoid creating pariah states. We are given a further opportunity to do this with NEW weapons. We can, and should, forge a world consensus that emphasizes the moral unacceptability, and therefore the cost in public opinion, from using weapons of this kind. Moral opprobrium is hardly a reliable barrier, but it has dissuasive power, particularly when it must be considered by terrorist groups seeking to establish the legitimacy of their cause.

Where dissuasive strategies do not succeed, we will, and should, rely on deterrent policies. However, strategies of deterrence must be extended and reworked to take account of the likelihood that terrorist groups and individuals are among potential users of NEW weapons. Deterring those actors (and their acquisition of NEW weaponry) is different from deterring state actors. We need to understand the psychology and structure of nonstate groups and recognize that old techniques (e.g. threats of nuclear retaliation) typically will not work against them.

When confronting terrorist groups (and some resolute second and third-tier states), disruption may be a more important strategy than deterrence. While deterrence threatens reaction, disruption is proactive: it intrudes upon would-be attackers, with preemptive strikes, inspections, arrests, or such pressure of detection and restriction on freedom of movement as to thwart intended strikes. Our society is uncomfortable with disruption: it threatens civil liberties, risks alienating public opinion (or creating martyrs) through heavy handedness, provides little assurance of success, and commits us to innumerable small battles without the likelihood of eradicating threats. It is, however, an essential tool against terrorism. We need to develop strategies of disruption that are closely controlled by civil authorities, narrowly targeted to thwart traumatic attacks by the least drastic means, and compliant with our own and international laws.

Beyond this, a fourth approach is needed to complement deterrence, dissuasion, and disruption – 'consequence management'. This approach would develop procedures and resources to limit the effects of attacks. Consequence management is required because our reliance on information systems will, over the next decades, persistently outrun our abilities to protect these systems completely. Similarly, biological, chemical, or explosive attacks will be so easily mounted, against targets so numerous and so exposed that society cannot be insulated completely against this trauma. Defense, dissuasion, deterrence, and disruption are worth substantial investment, but our working hypothesis ought to be that, despite our best efforts, successful traumatic attacks will occur.

Accordingly, we should invest in managing the consequences of attack so as to reduce the resulting trauma. By this means we will also diminish the incentive for opponents to utilize this form of attack. In the information context, this requires designing systems that are redundant and compartmentalized so that, when successfully attacked, failure is 'graceful' rather than catastrophic. It involves the design of data systems that are camouflaged to confuse intruders, tagged and encoded to detect manipulation, and encrypted to minimize the benefits of intrusion.

In biological defense, consequence management requires investments in our public health systems. We need standby medical capabilities so that attacks can be promptly recognized and therapeutic regimes initiated before symptoms become pernicious. In both information and biological defense, consequence management must include the creation of public and military information systems to diminish panic and confusion.

Such an approach to consequence management must also carry with it a rethinking of the anachronistic distinctions between 'here and abroad' and between military and civilians. Traumatic attacks that threaten our national security may be aimed at our troops and allies abroad, but they are as likely to be aimed at people and activities based in the United States. Certainly, cyberspace has no geography, and anyone who doubts that biological agents can easily be imported into the United States need look no further than the flow of drugs into this country. Once imported (or obtained), biological agents are easily disseminated by use of readily available crop sprayers and other such devices. Boundary defense cannot be relied upon to defend against cyber invasion or biological agents.

Investments in protecting civilians against these untraditional threats have a rationale and benefit not present when considering civilian protection against conventional weapons. Illness occurs naturally, and information security is challenged every day in our economy; therefore dollars used to protect us in these arenas yield everyday rewards. 'Civil defense' expenditures may be questioned, but by contrast, 'public health' investments (e.g., in the Centers for Disease Control and the Public Health Service) and information security investments are well warranted for coping with natural as well as military contingencies.

When dealing with NEW weapons, a line of separation cannot be drawn between military and civilian systems. Our ability to project military power depends, both here and abroad, on civilian utility, transport, telecommunications, and finance systems, which in turn depend on properly functioning civilian information systems and civilian employees. All can be undermined or overwhelmed by driving massive numbers of civilian populations away from or toward centers of activity. It is not likely that our response to a biological threat against Denver would, or should, be limited to the Denver Police Department, or even the FBI and Federal Emergency Management Agency. Nor could we ignore such threats against civilians in host nations that receive and sustain our forces when they are deployed abroad.

Sustaining our military power requires dealing with the consequences of traumatic attack. To do this we will have to focus on NEW weapons, in addition to explosive weapons; on terrorist groups and individuals, as well as major powers; on consequence management, as well as on defense, dissuasion, deterrence, and disruption; on civilians and civilian systems, not just military personnel and operations; and on our vulnerabilities at home as well as abroad.

NOTES

This study was originally published as part of *The Big Three: Our Greatest Security Risks and How to Address Them* (Washington DC: National Defense University 1999) pp.37–49.

1. Biological weapons are novel but not unprecedented. In the Middle Ages, bodies were catapulted over the walls of castles under siege in order to spread plague; in America's French and Indian Wars, Indians were given blankets infected with smallpox; in our Civil War, Sherman's March to the Sea was impeded by poisoned wells; and in World War II, Japanese Unit 731 experimented with biological weapons that killed as many as a thousand Chinese civilians.

    This subject is, for expository purposes, given limited space. Other types of NEW weapons should not be overlooked. Chemical weapons, the most pervasive and familiar, are somewhat more confined in their likely effects. They are also relatively easy to focus and control. Accordingly, they may be the most likely to be used. Radioactive weapons (though not necessarily explosive) lie at hand wherever there are large nuclear programs, whether developed for peaceful or military purposes. In Russia, perhaps the greatest source of risk in this regard, there are estimated to be some 2.5 million pounds of enriched uranium and plutonium. More than half of that is embedded in some 24,000 nuclear weapons, and 12,000 in storage. The balance of this weapons-grade material is in more than 50 military and civilian research institutes. With so little state power and economic well-being in Russia, there are high risks that this radioactive material will be bought or stolen and used for traumatic attack.

2. The appropriate absence of an offensive program and limited test information and experience make these estimates subject to debate.

3. *War and Anti-War: Survival at the Dawn of the 21st Century* (Boston: Little, Brown 1993).

4. Warfare of this kind is certainly not unprecedented. The Allied strategic bombing of Germany and America's use of atomic bombs against Japan were aimed, at least in part, at demoralizing our opponents.

Part Three

Where To From Here?

Deterrence and Competitive Strategies: A New Look at an Old Concept

ROBERT H. DORFF and JOSEPH R. CERAMI

Deterrence, as a concept, is hardly new. Though there is little research to support this claim early man probably practiced deterrence in the form of demonstrations of strength or prowess designed to deter the potential adversary from deciding to fight. As such, the concept of deterrence is simple: Actions undertaken to prevent another actor from doing that which it might otherwise do.[1] Subtleties of form and convoluted logic often cause us to lose sight of the relative simplicity of the concept.

The reasons for this complication of an otherwise simple concept are found in the modern (i.e., nuclear) age. The introduction of nuclear weapons and their potentially catastrophic destructive capabilities, coupled with the bipolar confrontation between the United States and the Soviet Union, created a unique security environment in which modern deterrence theory evolved. Deterrence became *de rigueur* in the 1950s and continued apace for nearly three decades thereafter. Terms such as first-strike and second-strike capabilities, counterforce and countervalue, extended and limited deterrence, and a host of others soon entered the lexicon. What often seemed like strange if not bizarre twists of logic were commonplace, such as the destabilizing tendencies of defense and the stabilizing influence of offense. An almost 'Alice in Wonderland' world of inverted and perverted logic (at least as seen by the non-experts in the field) dominated our thinking. This was especially true regarding 'unthinkable' scenarios involving mutually assured destruction (MAD).[2]

Our purpose in making these comments is not to disparage the concept of strategic nuclear deterrence. In fact, the Cold War approach to deterrence probably had much to do with keeping that war from becoming 'hot'. Rather, we wish to set the stage for our subsequent discussion of deterrence and competitive strategies by pointing out that we should return first to the essence of the concept of deterrence as we seek to evaluate its relevance and utility for the twenty-first century security environment. While some analyses will usefully evaluate the continued role of 'strategic nuclear deterrence', our purpose is to evaluate more generally the utility of deterrence as part of a forward-looking national security strategy for the new world that confronts us.

That this new world is replete with threats and challenges now seems obvious. This was not always the case. In the first few years following the end of the Cold War it was common to find optimistic assessments of the 'newly benign' security environment, and enthusiasm ran high for terms such as peace dividends, de-militarizing security, and the 'new world order'.

Today most recognize the shortsightedness of that thinking. Indeed, while the threat of global destruction through nuclear annihilation has declined perhaps to a near-zero probability, the number and diversity of threats have surely increased. Regional instability, rogue states, non-state actors, and continued WMD proliferation are just some of them. Although the downside of 'getting it wrong' may not be as great today as we thought it was during the height of the US–Soviet confrontation, the likelihood of 'getting it wrong' has increased as potentially threatening actors continue to multiply. Whereas deterrence served us well in managing the Soviet threat, the question now is whether it has anything to offer in dealing with rogue states, terrorists, and transnational organized crime.

We will argue that deterrence does have something important to offer to current security debates. Yet to see this we must not think only in terms limited to strategic nuclear deterrence. Instead, we have to return to some basics of deterrence and strategy. We also argue that thinking about deterrence in the context of competitive strategies, a term we will discuss in more detail shortly, offers a useful approach to analyzing the new threats and challenges. Of course, no approach offers a foolproof method for guaranteeing security. And the 'long peace' of the Cold War may have left us with somewhat unreasonable expectations about avoiding deterrence failure. However, the approach presented here offers a significantly better chance for success than simply trying to squeeze new threats into the old deterrence paradigm or throwing our hands up in despair and deciding to do nothing to deter the multiple threats emerging in the early twenty-first century.

We begin with some discussion of the basics and the essence of deterrence. Then we introduce the concept of competitive strategies. Following that we attempt to illustrate how the two can be combined in an approach to dealing with some of the 'non-traditional' security threats and challenges of the twenty-first century.

Deterrence

As noted in the introduction, deterrence involves getting another actor (usually an adversary but not necessarily) to choose not to do something it might otherwise do. In its classical formulation, then, deterrence is a relationship between actors based on perceptions of power. Moreover, and fundamentally, an actor *chooses* to be deterred. Deterrence does not simply exist on the basis of capabilities alone.[3] On the surface a simple concept, deterrence actually implies quite a lot in the way of substance and assumptions.

First, deterrence is directed against another actor.

Second, we try to deter that actor from a specific action. In other words, we do not just *deter*; rather, we deter *someone* from doing *something*.

Third, we assume or presume rationality on the part of this actor. An often misunderstood concept, rationality means only that the actor is able and willing to weigh the perceived costs of an action against the perceived benefits, and to choose a course of action that is logically related to the objectives and some reasonable cost-benefit ratio. That actor's objectives might appear quite 'irrational' or 'crazy' to us, but that is not the issue.[4] For deterrence to work, the actors must only engage in some logical assessment of the perceived costs and benefits of pursuing their objectives in the face of potential opposition.

A fourth element of the concept, and related to the assumption of rationality, is the view that for deterrence to work the communications between the actors must be clear and clearly understood. This adds complexity regarding the signaling and negotiating skills of diplomacy blending with the military instruments in order to make the potential 'costs' to the adversary clear and credible.

Fifth, we must have some kind of leverage over something the other actor values. Frequently this refers to the ability to credibly threaten something of value to that actor, but as we will discuss later, leverage may entail potential rewards as well as punishment. Also embedded in this is the notion that our threat to reward or punish is credible – that we actually have the means and the will to do what we say we will do. And finally, we assume that if not deterred, the other actor will in fact choose to do that which we wish it not to do.

These points are not merely academic or simply a matter of definitions. They have real meaning for the focus of this argument and indeed the entire special issue. If you cannot identify another actor to deter, the concept itself is of course meaningless. This is an especially important issue if we consider some of the potential non-state actors/adversaries in the system today.[5]

Moreover, if we cannot specify with some precision what it is that this actor might do, it will be difficult to tailor a specific deterrence policy to address it. So, whereas deterring state-supported terrorism might fall neatly into the framework of traditional deterrence, deterring terrorist activities that are not state-supported may require us to do considerably more thinking about the who and the what questions.

And once identified, if that actor is truly not rational, then the deterrence framework may once again be inappropriate and perhaps even dangerous (as we fool ourselves into thinking that it will work). Certain non-state actors (so-called 'fanatical' terrorist groups) and rogue-states (ruled by so-called 'crazy' tyrants) are often characterized in this fashion.[6]

In the contemporary debate about the utility of deterrence and its relevance to some of these non-traditional threats and challenges, the importance of communication has been somewhat underplayed. Our consideration here of assumptions and premises helps us to see that we should at least consider more carefully the questions related to what we wish to communicate and how we should communicate it. And recent research and analysis indicates that there may in fact be more points of potential leverage over these kinds of actors than we have previously thought, but we have to spend the time and effort required to identify them more effectively. And of course, we can always invest more resources in efforts to deter 'bad things' from happening. If there is no identifiable *something* that a *specifiable actor intends to do*, we will be hard-pressed to find the appropriate ways and means to prevent it. These are serious issues, and they raise important questions that deterrence strategies should address.

Consider three interesting dimensions of this challenge.

First, we must focus with some precision on the linkage between the ways we choose to deter and the specific action that we wish to deter. We discovered this in the 1950s with Massive Retaliation as the basis of US national military strategy. The concept as originally presented in 1954 by Secretary of State Dulles presumed that the threat of nuclear retaliation by the United States could deter all potential adversaries from using military force across the entire conflict spectrum. Subsequent analysis and events proved this to be quite wrong, mostly for reasons encapsulated in our brief list above. For one thing, US policymakers presumed that the only actor they needed to deter was the Soviet Union, and that Moscow controlled all the other actors in the system. So they answered the *who* question inadequately.

Second, they assumed that the US threat of nuclear retaliation was equally credible for all possible threats to US interests. The threat of Massive Retaliation would prevent a communist insurgency just as effectively as it would prevent a Soviet nuclear strike against the US mainland. This kind of thinking failed to specify the *what* they wished to deter, and to link it effectively to the *how* (in order to maximize the perceived credibility of the deterrent threat).

The second dimension we want to address here concerns the use of scarce resources to address security risks. If we do not carefully analyze and consider both the capabilities and the intentions of the actor, we can easily waste substantial resources on a strategy designed to deter an actor from doing that which they have no intention of doing. This is an invitation for an adversary to draw us into a wasteful and altogether meaningless use of those scarce resources.

The third dimension we wish to highlight is the importance of time. We must recall that in any deterrence strategy, the objective is to deter the undesired behavior over time and not just at that moment. This suggests that we may have to shift among different elements of power and different combinations of them in order to ensure the continued deterrence of the adversary. Moreover, it suggests that we must constantly reassess over time our objectives, the means we have at our disposal, and the ways in which we use them. The adversary may change its strategy and we must be capable of adjusting in a timely fashion.

What these three dimensions of the challenge suggest for security generally, and for the role of deterrence specifically, is that we should be very specific about the actor and the action we propose to deter, and how we can best accomplish that deterrence over time.

Approaches to Deterrence

Assuming that the conditions and assumptions noted above hold, we can approach deterrence in one of two general ways: By punishment and by denial. Deterrence by punishment is the classical approach in which one informs the adversary that the undesired action, if undertaken, will be met with a severe response. This is the obvious conditional threat of punishment: 'If you do X, then I will punish you by doing Y.' The essential idea is that the adversary, weighing the potential cost of punishment against the potential benefit of the action if undertaken, would rationally decide to forgo the action. Clearly, we must know who the other actor is and what action we wish to deter – not only to devise the deterrent in the first place, but also to communicate the threat of punishment clearly and unambiguously.

That threat may be either explicit or implicit; the point is simply that the other actor must understand the threat and its relationship to the undesired action. The threat must address something the other actor values or the all-important rational cost-benefit analysis will not lead to the desired decision.[7] And of course, the threat must be credible, so we must possess both the necessary tangible capabilities (e.g., weapons) and intangible intentions (e.g., will to use them).

Deterrence by punishment is obviously the primary underpinning of the US–Soviet 'balance of terror' or MAD that has become nearly synonymous with deterrence generally. Each side held the population of its adversary 'hostage' to the destructive capacity of thermonuclear weapons. Defensive measures undertaken by either side were potentially destabilizing because they threatened to alter the cost-benefit calculations of a preemptive strike; if you could protect your population from a retaliatory strike, the threatened punishment meant nothing. Improved capabilities for destroying the adversary's population were potentially stabilizing as they reinforced the 'assured' component of MAD. The key was to maintain the 'mutual' component; as long as both sides valued their respective populations, and as long as each side could assure an 'unacceptable level' of destruction of the adversary's population, neither side had a rational reason for striking first.

The preoccupation with strategic nuclear deterrence has caused analysts to miss some important aspects of deterrence thinking. For example, consider the following two aspects. First, there is no necessary presumption of punishment by military force (although most of the literature is preoccupied with that element of power).

Second, there is a clear flip side to deterrence by punishment that we might call *deterrence by reward*. As long as the relationship meets the essential conditions described above, the threatened response can take many forms and employ a variety of elements of power. Consequently, the cost-benefit analysis should be conducted broadly and include economic, political and social dimensions. For example, the threat of trade sanctions may under certain circumstances provide just as credible and effective a basis for deterrence as the threat of a military response. In some instances it may even provide a more credible and effective deterrent.

Similarly, the promise of rewards for not undertaking the action may provide sufficient inducement for the other actor to accept deterrence. If an actor values the reward sufficiently (i.e., more than the perceived value of the action we wish to deter), then that actor will make the choice to be deterred. If deterrence is the result of a perceived power relationship between two actors, then there are no *a priori* limits on the kinds of power involved (military, political, economic), nor any implied exclusive reliance on punishment rather than reward.

This broader interpretation of deterrence is hardly new, but some seem to have lost sight of it as a result of the fixation on strategic nuclear deterrence. Consider for example a classical presentation on the subject written by Glenn Snyder in 1961. At that time Snyder wrote:

> One deters another party from doing something by the implicit or explicit threat of applying some sanction if the forbidden act is performed, or by the promise of a reward if the act is not performed. Thus conceived, deterrence does not have to depend on military force. We might speak of deterrence by the threat of trade restrictions, for example. The promise of economic aid might deter a country from

military action (or any action) contrary to one's own interests ... In short, deterrence may follow, first, from any form of control which one has over an opponent's present and prospective 'value inventory'; secondly, from the communication of a credible threat or promise to decrease or increase that inventory; and, thirdly, from the opponent's degree of confidence that one intends to fulfill the threat or promise.[8]

In Snyder's formulation we see once again the simple essence of deterrence: getting the adversary to decide not to do something. Precisely what we do to cause this decision by the adversary is less relevant to the basic concept of deterrence than we might at first think.

Snyder's more general formulation also helps us to understand deterrence by denial. If deterrence results from a power relationship based on these calculations of perceived costs and benefits (effects on the 'value inventory' as he calls it), then there should be other ways to alter that relationship. Deterrence by denial refers to one's ability to deny the other actor the ability to so influence one's own value inventory. So, for example, in military terms, if I can adequately defend my population against another country's retaliatory strike, the basis of strategic nuclear deterrence disappears. I am freed up to do whatever I choose to do, and I will conceivably choose not to be deterred. If I can remove the item I value from my credibly threatened value inventory (either by sufficiently reducing its value to me or by sufficiently reducing my adversary's ability to credibly threaten it), I can alter the cost-benefit ratio and in theory 'escape' from the deterrence relationship. Conversely, perhaps I can find other things to move into my adversary's credibly threatened value inventory through careful analysis and planning.

So, deterrence by denial may entail a wide array of possible options, but it will certainly include the reduction of my own valued vulnerabilities (deny the adversary the opportunity of exploiting them) and the reduction of the adversary's ability to exploit my valued vulnerabilities (deny the adversary the ways and means with which to exploit them).

It is also important to recognize that deterrence need not be mutual. There is no necessary reciprocity in a deterrence relationship; my ability to deter my adversary does not imply that my adversary can deter me. Only in the unique circumstances of MAD was this the case, and the striving for the achievement and maintenance of mutual deterrence was itself a matter of choice. And each side wanted the other to continue to choose that option, hence the search for equilibrium for this system of mutual deterrence. While each side planned for the possibilities of deterrence failure, they also undertook measures to ensure stable vulnerabilities. Viewed in this light, the Anti-Ballistic Missile Treaty (1972) seemed to make a great deal of sense at the time, as did limits on numbers of warheads and other technological improvements (the qualitative part of the arms race). The objective was to avoid nuclear devastation through the mutual deterrence of the two superpowers, and to ensure the avoidance of an unconstrained arms race whose outcome would ultimately be catastrophic.

Deterrence Fallacies

Two simple schools of thought about deterrence have emerged in the aftermath of both the Cold War and the initial euphoria that set in.

One is the simple view that our nuclear arsenal should be adequate for deterring all serious threats to the US and its interests. Therefore, we should do everything we can to maintain and develop further the technological superiority we possess. No actor (state or non-state) would be 'foolish' enough to risk the consequences of punishment inflicted upon it by the US with its nuclear arsenal. This school frequently comes very close to the fallacy of 'existential deterrence' discussed earlier.

The second school sees nuclear weapons as completely irrelevant for the kinds of threats we face, and they reject not only the relevance of nuclear weapons but also the relevance of deterrence. In effect, they come very close to throwing the baby (deterrence) out with the bath water (nuclear weapons). We cannot deter rogue states, so this logic goes, because they have 'crazy' leaders and the people cannot control them through our kinds of democratic processes.

Terrorists are certainly not rational, so we cannot deter them. And these new, non-state actors do not even possess the normal structures of governments, so how can we possibly threaten them or things that they value? And how could we even think of using nuclear weapons in reprisal if that use entails mass casualties among innocent bystanders?

The problem is that we have some serious shortcomings in the strategic thinking underlying these admittedly simplified views. Strategy is the relationship of ends (objectives), ways (concepts), and means (resources). How do we best use the available means to pursue our objectives? In our view much, if not all, of this thinking gets us off track by confusing a strategic concept (deterrence) with the means (nuclear weapons). Recall our earlier discussion. We deter a specific actor from undertaking a specific action in order to achieve some specific objective (non-use of nuclear weapons, preservation of peace, avoidance of war, etc.). Deterrence is not an objective in and of itself, although we often spoke during the Cold War of achieving and maintaining deterrence as though it were. Rather, deterrence is one way of achieving an objective. Strategic nuclear deterrence, and especially MAD, was a specific way of using a specific means (nuclear weapons) to achieve a larger strategic objective. Viewed in this way, it is then even more apparent that there must be different means we can use in different ways (including in combination) against different actors to deter different actions.

Competitive Strategies

Before we turn to our discussion of how this broader application of deterrence applies to the contemporary security environment, we introduce one final element into the framework: competitive strategies.[9] Although we cannot explore this overall approach in any detail here, we do need to introduce some of its essential components along with a little background.[10] According to David Andre, competitive strategies grew out of some of the earliest analyses of the US-Soviet competition conducted during the late 1940s, but it only began to take on distinct characteristics as a planning process and methodology with the work of Andrew W. Marshall in the 1960s and early 1970s.[11] It gained public attention beginning in 1986 when Secretary of Defense Caspar W. Weinberger oversaw the design and implementation of the DoD Competitive Strategies Initiative.[12]

Several elements of the competitive strategies approach differ substantially from the typical US strategy planning processes.

First, the approach focuses on specific, long-term competitions with specific competitors. Although the US might be engaged in multiple competitions with multiple competitors, this approach requires looking at each one individually. Broad strategic guidelines may be possible, but a 'one-size-fits-all' strategy is unlikely to succeed.

Second, the approach forces the strategic thinking to focus on specific, actionable objectives in the context of that specific competition. What can we accomplish in our competition with this specific competitor?

Third, the approach emphasizes 'exploiting our strengths in leveraging [a competitor's] weaknesses and vulnerabilities'.[13]

Fourth, by virtue of its broader approach to defining competition and competitors, and its emphasis on leveraging comparative strengths against comparative weaknesses, it naturally encourages a focus on a wider array of national elements of power. Relying solely on the military element unnecessarily restricts the successful exploitation of strengths over weaknesses. In a specific competition, the military element may be more or less relevant and potentially effective than the economic or political elements. Choosing the appropriate element and instruments is clearly a critical part of formulating the strategy.

Andre's subsequent discussion of how they applied this approach to the US-Soviet competition is quite informative. Department of Defense (DoD) analysts examined Soviet predispositions as part of the inventory of the adversary's strengths and weaknesses. The DoD group then set out to find specific ways to accomplish the following:

- Encourage the Soviets to divert resources to less threatening forces or doctrine (e.g., defensive rather than offensive capabilities);

- Get them to preserve forces we could defeat relatively easily (e.g., fixed-site air defenses);

- Outdate existing Soviet capabilities (i.e., impose costs; for example, by regularly modernizing our air forces);

- Establish areas of enduring military competence (e.g., use our doctrine, operational concepts, technology, etc., to shape the competition);

- Present unanticipated military capabilities with potentially significant impacts on the Soviets (i.e., take the initiative, shift the focus of the competition, and change the rules of the game);

- Make the Soviets uncertain about the effectiveness of major components of their military capability (e.g., doctrine, plans, existing equipment, R&D program, etc.) or otherwise undermine their confidence in the expected outcome of their plans and programs.[14]

The specific content of the devised strategy is not important for our discussion. From these general objectives one can see the essence of a competitive strategies approach. There is a specific competitor with specific strengths and weaknesses. Our objectives are a function of that specific competition and what we seek to accomplish in it. Our strategy should attempt to exploit the competitor's weaknesses, especially by applying our strengths most effectively in pursuit of our objectives. And we must recognize that all of this is part of a competitive relationship over time, and probably a long time.[15]

Competitive Strategies, Deterrence, and Contemporary Threats

How can we apply these two concepts, deterrence and competitive strategies, to the contemporary security environment? In our view it is precisely the complexity and ambiguity of the current security environment that make a competitive strategies approach absolutely essential for our security planning. The diversity of actors and the potential threats associated with them suggest that a 'one-size-fits-all' strategy simply will not suffice. How we approach our competitions with Russia and China will not be the same, and how we approach those kinds of competition will surely differ from that of North Korea or Iraq. How we address the threats and challenges of current and future nuclear states will surely differ from how we address those that emanate from terrorism. And we daresay that not all terrorist threats and challenges are the same either.

A forward-looking strategy for the twenty-first century must begin with the recognition of this diversity, and it must attempt to incorporate that diversity in the overall strategic planning. We must identify the most important competitions, search for the specific and most crucial characteristics of that competition (including those of the specific competitor), and then devise specific and attainable objectives for that competition over time. Acknowledging that a competitive strategies approach compels us to do just that is an important first step in the process.

A second important step is to acknowledge that deterrence, as one among many general ways to accomplish our specific objectives, is alive and well, but it is not simply the deterrence we knew in the Cold War, preoccupied with and based almost exclusively on nuclear weapons. Nor is it deterrence based solely on threatened punishment by military means. Once again, the diversity of the actors and the threats and challenges they pose suggest that we must broaden the potential tools and the ways in which we use them *in order to induce the adversary into choosing to be deterred.* This is, after all, the ultimate objective of deterrence. To do that, as we discussed earlier, requires us to know much more precisely who it is we want to deter from doing what. This suggests that deterrence, when combined with a competitive strategies approach, has much to offer as we gaze upon the still-unfolding contemporary security environment. Some brief illustrations should help make this point.

Consider the case of North Korea and US efforts to prevent it from becoming a nuclear weapons state. In 1994 the North Korean government announced that it would withdraw from the Nuclear Non-Proliferation Treaty (NPT). It was violating its earlier pledge to allow its nuclear facilities to be inspected, and the US government was reasonably certain that the North Koreans had already diverted 'at least a bomb's worth' of fissionable material.[16] When North Korea chose a confrontational response to the US threat of sanctions, the US reversed course and negotiated the now all-too-familiar nuclear reactor deal in return for a North Korean pledge to freeze its 'declared nuclear activities and eventually uphold its non-proliferation inspection pledges sometime after the year 2000'.[17] Since that time, we have found ourselves on more than one occasion caught in a kind of trap in which North Korea refuses to do something and we have to up the ante. Why?

We think the answer is fairly simple: The US chose a 'losing' strategy.[18]

First, we apparently lost sight of the strategic objective, which was to prevent North Korea from becoming a nuclear weapons state. Instead, we substituted (perhaps unknowingly and without reflection) the objective of keeping them from withdrawing from the NPT.

Second, instead of seeking to deter them from the undesired behavior we actually rewarded them for that behavior. By offering a 'good deal' in return for their promise not to continue in that direction, we actually established a relationship in which they could periodically go back to the undesired behavior and expect additional increases in the rewards. Consistent with our earlier discussion of deterrence by reward, note that we could have offered to reward them for choosing not to pursue a nuclear weapons program. However, that is quite different from the approach the US actually chose, which was in fact to reward them precisely for the behavior.

From a deterrence perspective we failed to think carefully about the North Korean 'value inventory' and the potential leverage we had over it. What does North Korea and its leadership fundamentally value or need that we could potentially increase or decrease?

From a competitive strategies perspective, we ceded leverage to them over us when it was completely unnecessary. Moreover, we failed to look at the specific competitor and competition, and to plan our strategy accordingly. As Sokolski observes more generally, '...there is no substitute for non-proliferation strategies with clear, country-specific objectives'.[19]

Casting non-proliferation objectives in sweeping global terms, and trying to pursue those objectives in similarly sweeping form and fashion (international regimes and unenforceable treaties) may sound good, but as we have recently seen again with India and Pakistan, it rarely works. Those who wish to pursue proliferation will do so unless confronted by an effectively designed approach to deter them from making that choice. We can do this by 'orchestrating persistent, tailored, leveraging actions with our friends that move better governments toward the right choices and keep the worst from making the wrong ones'.[20]

We can argue in much the same way about terrorism. Despite the considerable volume of work focusing on the differences between non-state (and non-state-supported) terrorism and traditional state actors, a competitive strategies approach employing deterrence as one of perhaps several ways to accomplish our objectives has considerable merit.

First, it should lead us to see that not all terrorists are the same. We must seek an understanding of the specific terrorist group and the nature of its competition with us. This involves especially an understanding of the group's objectives, and its strategy for achieving them. Recent work in this area suggests that not all terrorist groups are particularly dangerous to us, and that only some demonstrate a realistic potential for using weapons of mass destruction (WMD).[21]

Second, we need to look more carefully for the underlying 'value inventory' of such organizations. Most terrorists and terrorist organizations have things that they value, including access to their audience, attention and recognition, and so on. Accurately identifying the key elements of this value inventory is essential to the competitive strategies/deterrence approach. Questions we need to ask include the following examples: What are the objectives of the group? Are those objectives fundamentally in conflict with our own, or can we seek accommodation? What are those things that the group and/or its leaders value that we can possibly leverage? Does the group pose a threat of using unacceptable means (WMD)? What is it we need to deter them from doing and how can we best accomplish this over time?

Conclusions

This discussion here of a single rogue state and terrorism is obviously quite general, and we do not mean to imply that dealing with either rogue states or terrorists will be easy if only we adopt this approach. As Colin Gray observed at the conference that led to this collection, 'deterrence is difficult because strategy is difficult to do'.[22] Competitive strategies is an approach to 'doing strategy' that may at first glance seem to make the enterprise all that more difficult. For example, there are 14 key questions that the approach says we must answer in order to develop a sound strategy, and none of those 14 questions is simple and easy to answer. Yet the approach does help analysts to raise the right questions, to focus on a specific actor and a specific competition, and to consider creative ways in which to leverage comparative strengths against comparative weaknesses over time. By doing this, the competitive strategies approach may be just what we need in our attempts to address the challenges of the still-emerging and highly complex security environment of the twenty-first century.

Deterrence in its more general sense also has much to offer the strategist in dealing with the myriad threats and challenges in today's security environment. It is especially valuable when viewed through the lenses of a competitive strategies approach – not as a single concept to be applied universally, but as one part of an overall strategy tailored to a specific competition with an identifiable competitor. This means that there is still a role for strategic nuclear deterrence, especially in managing parts of US ongoing competitions with countries such as Russia and China. We should also view deterrence as entailing the use of both 'carrots and sticks', and not simply or solely in terms of 'punishment.'

Moreover, we should broaden our consideration and use of the elements of power as we seek to deter. The military element is only one of the four we can constructively employ as we seek to deter the competitor from a specific action or policy.[23] As this discussion has highlighted, most of what is required for deterrence to be a useful strategic concept is for the adversary to have a 'value inventory' and for us to be able to leverage it effectively.[24] We suggest that the conditions necessary for deterrence to be effective exist in a much broader array of potential relationships than is commonly argued, including with rogue states and their leaders, and even with terrorist organizations and other non-state actors. If we use them properly, deterrence and competitive strategies should provide some essential components for a forward-looking national security strategy for the twenty-first century.

NOTES

1. There are, of course, several variations on this simple definition.
2. See of course, Herman Kahn, *Thinking About the Unthinkable* (NY: Horizon Press 1962).
3. This is what Colin Gray has called the fallacy of existential deterrence: 'My nuclear weapons exist, therefore they deter.' In a most fundamental sense, deterrence is a mutual state of mind because it exists only when two actors choose to believe it does, and to adjust their behavior accordingly.
4. A useful and informative discussion of rationality from this perspective is David Jablonsky, *Strategic Rationality Is Not Enough: Hitler and the Concept of Crazy States* (Carlisle Barracks, PA: US Army War College, Strategic Studies Inst. 1991). See esp. Chs. 2 and 7.
5. Consider the frequent references to how difficult it would be to retaliate against a non-state actor such as a terrorist group that cannot be clearly identified (either in terms of who it is or where it is).
6. We will argue below that some of the thinking about deterrence has been limited by weak analysis concerning the rationality of non-state and rogue state actors.
7. Jablonsky makes this point in discussing the 'crazy state'. He argues that '...there must be some appreciation of the fundamental values of a crazy state, no matter how bizarre in Western perceptions, if there is to be effective deterrence. Without this appreciation, deterrence may be attempted by threatening punishment directed at values which, while important to the deterring nation, may be quite irrelevant to the crazy state' (p.73). But of course this is equally true in the general sense: For deterrence to work, we must be able to threaten credibly something the other actor values.
8. Glenn H. Snyder, *Deterrence and Defense: Toward a Theory of National Security* (Princeton, NJ: Princeton UP 1961) pp.9–10.
9. For a useful overview of the approach in the context of proliferation, see David J. Andre, 'Competitive Strategies: An Approach Against Proliferation', in Henry Sokolski (ed.), *Fighting Proliferation: New Concerns for the Nineties* (Maxwell Air Force Base, AL: Air UP 1996).
10. The specific term, competitive strategies, has been used by Andrew W. Marshall, Michael E. Porter, David J. Andre, and others. The term itself is less important than the approach and its applications. Therefore, we concentrate on the aspects of the approach most relevant for our discussion. See Andre (note 9) for a more detailed description and additional references.
11. See A.W. Marshall, *Long-Term Competition with the Soviets: A Framework for Strategic Analysis* (U), RAND Report R-862-PR (Santa Monica, CA: RAND, April 1972).
12. As reported in Andre (note 9) pp.259–60, the announcement of this initiative is contained in the *Annual Report to the Congress, Fiscal Year 1987* (Washington DC: Govt Printing Office 1986). It was more officially titled *Competitive Strategies for the Long-Term Competition with the Soviet Union*.
13. Andre (note 9) p.258.
14. Ibid. pp.262–3.
15. This is by no means a full and complete description of the competitive strategies approach.

For that we refer the reader to Andre (note 9). We have highlighted only those components necessary for making our subsequent arguments. But other aspects of the approach are quite important to the current discussion. For example, it suggests that we must look at relevant third parties to the competition. Consider how such third parties have historically contributed to the effectiveness of economic sanctions (by making them either more or less porous). It also requires the analyst to think through the potential countermoves of the competitor, and to plan against them.

16. Most of this is widely known and substantiated in a host of public sources. Our summary relies on the cogent overview and analysis provided by Henry Sokolski, 'Faking It and Making It', *The National Interest* No. 51 (Spring 1998) pp.67–74.
17. Ibid. p.67.
18. See Henry Sokolski, 'Nonproliferation: Strategies for Winning, Losing and Coping', unpublished manuscript available from the Nonproliferation Policy Education Center, Washington DC.
19. Sokolski (note 16) p.74.
20. Ibid. Together with the Nonproliferation Policy Education Center, and with the support of the Institute for National Security Studies at the US Air Force Academy, some of us at the US Army War College will conduct two workshops in summer 2000 focusing on a competitive strategies approach for North Korea. The goal is to formulate a strategy using the competitive strategies approach.
21. Work by Daniel S. Gressang IV is perhaps most characteristic of this recent work. He argues that 'all terrorists are alike in at least one fundamental way: they seek to acquire and maintain some degree of influence over an identifiable audience'. Building on that, he is able to construct a framework for assessing the likelihood that a specific terrorist group will actually use WMD. Critical to his argument is the assumption of rationality much as presented here. They have a preference order and are preference maximizers. In the language of deterrence they, too, have a 'value inventory' although it may differ substantially from our own. See Gressang, 'Audience and Message: Assessing Terrorist WMD Potential'. (Paper presented at the Annual Convention of the International Studies Association, Los Angeles, CA, 14–18 March 2000.) Cited with permission of author.
22. Research Conference, 'Deterrence in the 21st Century', Center for Strategic Leadership, US Army War College, 8–9 Dec. 1999.
23. There are four elements of power if one accepts the notion that information is a separate element along with the military, political, and economic elements.
24. Stating it this way also implies that the other key components we discussed (rationality, communications, credibility, etc.) also apply.

The Challenge of Preventive Diplomacy and Deterrence in the Global Security Environment: Applying the 'Iron Fist' within the 'Velvet Glove' Now and in the Future

EDWIN G. CORR and MAX G. MANWARING

Over the years, particularly since the beginning of World War II, national security has been viewed as protection from external attack, and thought of largely in terms of military defenses against military threats. Yet, given the opportunities and threats inherent in the predominantly interdependent global security environment, that is clearly too narrow a conception. American security today involves such more than the procurement and application of military forces. Thus, this conclusion espouses a 'new' forward looking, proactive, civil-military approach to national security that combines the potent virtues of the proverbial military 'iron fist' within the diplomatic 'velvet glove'.

The Search for Security in the Contemporary Global Security Environment

The demise of the Soviet Union has left the United States as the preeminent world political, economic, and military power, and invested us with unparalleled leadership responsibilities in terms of maintaining and enhancing the new world order from which we profit so well. The end of military superpower competition has also eliminated George Kennan's unifying 'containment' approach to national security. Now, in addition to traditional regional security issues, an array of non-traditional threats – from proliferation of weapons of mass destruction, regional ethnic and religious conflict, a hundred different varieties of terrorism, and criminal anarchy to completely non-military threats such as trade war, financial war, new terror war (e.g., the improving sophistication in using chemical and biological agents), and cyber war – challenge the United States at home and abroad, and blurs the old Cold War dividing lines between military, political, and economic security affairs.

The Need for a Paradigm Change

Perhaps the greatest threat to US national security is the danger that we Americans do not easily change our thinking to coincide with the changes in the world around us. America's principal defense priority for more than 40 years was the management of low-probability, high-intensity nuclear conflict, with a primary focus on Europe. Yet ironically, nearly all the armed conflicts during that time took place in the Third World and were classified as low intensity. With the exception of the Korean conflict and the tragic Vietnam experience – and in large part because of it – we Americans during the Cold War were slow to adapt our thinking, organization, and resource allocations to high-probability, low-intensity conflict, in which our military's role is usually relatively small and indirect, and extraordinary support is required for civilian authorities in development efforts.

In the national security establishment, the planning focus has been on the high end of the conflict spectrum, while for some years US civil-military forces have been increasingly engaged in operations at the lower end of the conflict scale, such as peace operations, humanitarian and disaster assistance, and counter-narcotics and anti-terrorism operations. World leadership now and in the future depends on a different set of assets and resources than it did during the Cold War era of military superpower confrontations. In the national security establishment, policy-makers are searching for new strategies.

The United States faces a challenge to change perspectives. We need an organizing paradigm to assist us in clarifying our global leadership role, and our purposes and courses of action. One message is unmistakable. The emerging global order has given the United States the longest period of economic prosperity anyone in the current generation can remember, but the end of the Cold War era conflict did not signal the end of all global conflict. Indeed, just the reverse is proving to be true. If we want to preserve the present prosperity and continue to benefit from it, we must pay for it and nurture it. Thus, US interests, and the fragile and interdependent global community, demand a peace enforcer – an iron fist encased in a velvet glove.

This does not mean that the United States must be involved all over the world all the time. It does mean, however, that the United States must rethink and renew the concept of deterrence. In much the same way that Kennan's Containment Theory of Engagement was conceived in 1947, philosophical underpinnings must be devised for a new policy to deal with more diverse threats – from unpredictable directions – and by more diverse state and non-state actors.

Some Additional Considerations that Help Define Threat and Dictate Response

When we think about the possibilities of conflict, we tend to invent for ourselves a comfortable US-centric vision – a situation with battlefields that are well understood, with an enemy who looks and acts more or less as we do, and a situation in which the fighting is done by the military. We must recognize, however, that in protecting our interests and confronting and influencing an adversary today, the situation has changed. We can see that change in several ways.

1. Ambiguity. First, the definition of 'enemy' and 'victory' is elusive and the use of 'power' against an enemy to achieve some form of success is diffuse. Underlying these ambiguities is the fact that most contemporary conflict tends to be an intra-state affair (i.e., not an issue between sovereign states) that international law and convention is only beginning to address. It is one part or several parts of one society against another. Thus, there are virtually no rules. In these wars there is normally no formal declaration or termination of conflict, no easily identifiable enemy military formations to attack and destroy, no specific territory to take and hold, no single credible government or political actor with which to deal, no legal niceties such as mutually recognized national borders and Geneva Conventions to help control the situation, no guarantee that any agreement between or among contending authorities will be honored, and no commonly accepted rules of engagement to guide the leadership of a given international 'peacekeeping' organization.

2. The Need to Redefine 'Enemy', 'Power' and 'Victory'. Second, the ambiguous political-psychological-moral nature of contemporary conflict forces the redefinition of long-used terms. The enemy is no longer a recognizable military entity or an industrial capability to make war. The enemy now becomes the individual actor that plans and implements violence, and exploits the causes of violence. Power is no longer simply combat firepower directed at a traditional enemy military soldier or industrial complex. Power is multi-level and combined political, psychological, moral, informational, economic, social, military, police, and civil bureaucratic activity that can be brought to bear appropriately on the causes as well as the perpetrators of violence. And, victory is no longer the obvious and acknowledged destruction of military capability, and the resultant 'unconditional' surrender. Victory, or success, is now – more and more, and perhaps with a bit of 'spin control' – defined as the achievement of 'peace'.

3. A 'New' Center of Gravity. These ambiguities intrude on the 'comfortable' vision of war in which the assumed center of gravity has been enemy military formations and his physical capability to conduct war. Clausewitz reminds us, however, that in places subject to internal strife, the hub of all power and strength (i.e., center of gravity) is leadership and public opinion. It is against these that our energies should be directed. Thus, in contemporary intra-national conflict, the primary center of gravity changes from a familiar military concept to an ambiguous and uncomfortable leadership and public opinion paradigm.

4. Conflict Has Become Multi-organizational, Multi-lateral, and Multi-dimensional. Fourth, conflict is no longer a simple military to military confrontation. Conflict now involves entire populations. Conflict now involves a large number of indigenous national civilian agencies, other national civilian organizations, international organizations, non-governmental organizations, private voluntary organizations, and sub-national indigenous actors involved in dealing politically, economically, socially, morally, or militarily with complex threats to international security and well-being. And, those are just the 'good guys'. The number and diversity of 'bad guy' players can be as large. As a consequence, an almost unheard of unity of effort is required to coordinate the multi-lateral, multi-dimensional, and multi-organizational paradigm necessary for success on either or all sides of a contemporary conflict. That ideal has not often been achieved in the past. Nevertheless, in the new and infinitely more complex situation, governments and various other actors involved in such endeavors must find ways and means to work more effectively together.

5. Contemporary Conflict is Not Limited; It is Total. Finally, contemporary non-traditional war is not a kind of appendage – a lesser or limited thing – to the comfortable vision of war. It is a great deal more. As long as opposition exists that is willing to risk everything to violently take down a government, destroy a society, or cause great harm to a society – there is war. This is a zero-sum game in which there is only one winner. It is, thus, total.   This is the case with other governments, rogue states, Maoist insurgents, Osama bin Ladin's terrorists, the Japanese Aum Shinrikyo cult, Mafia families, Southeast Asian warlords, or Serbian ethnic cleansers – among others.

This is also the case with the deliberate 'financial war' attack planned and implemented by owners of international mobile capital that generated the Southeast Asia financial crisis and inflicted devastating injury on Asia's 'little tiger' countries. Their non-military financial actions caused socio-economic-political devastation that could not have been exceeded by a regional war. This is also the case with the systems analyst, software engineer, scholar, or 16-year-old 'hacker' that can impair the security of an army or a nation electronically as seriously as a nuclear bomb. Finally, as one more example, it must be remembered that Germany's former Chancellor, Helmut Kohl, breached the Berlin Wall with the powerful Deutschmark – not aircraft, artillery, armor, or infantry.

These are the deterrence realities for the twenty-first century. Everything else is illusion.

Deterrence and Preventive Diplomacy

In the anarchic environment of global politics, regardless of perceived intent, what one state or political actor does will inevitably impinge on another. That action will affect some beneficially, others adversely. Mutual dependence means that each political actor must take others into account. Interdependence affects nothing more powerfully than it does security. The result can be a vicious downward action-reaction spiral that takes the global community into instability, violence, chaos, and the inevitable destruction of stability, peace, and prosperity. As a consequence, political actors have always tried to deter others from engaging in activities considered to be harmful, or to encourage actions thought to be beneficial. A major problem in all this is that the anarchic environment of global politics allows each political actor to be the only and the final judge of his interests and actions.

The Primary Rules

Here is where preventive diplomacy comes into play. The general rule would be that decision-makers and policy-makers must carefully calculate possible gains and losses, and when the case warrants, apply pre-planned indirect and direct deterrent measures earlier rather than later. If done earlier, this implies the initial and intense use of low-cost diplomatic and civilian resources and military support units to ensure the deterrence message has adequate back-up. If applied earlier, preventive measures may reduce tensions that if left to fester could lead to deadly results. If done later, this normally implies the initial and intense use of high-cost military combat units to respond to a losing situation. If applied later, preventive measures may turn out to be either irrelevant or counter-productive.

Ultimately, however, the only viable test for indirect or direct preventive action sooner or later is national self-interest. In any case, the basic logic of the application of preventive diplomacy is unassailable – the sooner the better.

Deterrence, then, is not necessarily military – although that is important. It is not necessarily negative or directly coercive – although that, too, is important. Deterrence is much broader than that. Deterrence can be direct and/or indirect political-diplomatic, socio-economic, psychological-moral, and/or military-coercive. In its various forms and combinations of forms, it is an attempt to influence how and what an enemy or potential enemy thinks and does. That is, deterrence is the creation of a state of mind that either discourages one thing, or encourages something else. Motives and culture, thus, become crucial. It is in this context that political-military communication – and preventive diplomacy – become a vital part of the deterrence equation.

Intermediate Rules

In that context, the deterrence 'rule of thumb' must move from US-centric values, and determine precisely what a hostile leadership values most. The 'deterrer' must then determine precisely what a hostile leadership values most – and identify exactly how that cultural 'thing' – whatever it is – can realistically be held at risk. Conversely, a new deterrence 'rule of thumb' must also consider what a hostile leadership values most and – as opposed to the proverbial 'stick' – identify precisely what 'carrots' might also be offered as deterrents.

In the chaos of the 'new world disorder,' the threat of devastating attacks on the US and its interests at home and abroad perpetrated by the Russian Federation, China, and other nuclear powers still retains a certain credibility. As a result, the deterrence and preventive diplomacy task is to get into the minds of these diverse political actors, and to find viable ways and means of convincing them NOT to use nuclear or any other kind of weapons against us or anybody else in the global community.

Moreover, the threats associated with the growing sophistication of biological and chemical war, and cyber war, are intensifying. At the same time, other 'non-traditional' threats and menaces emanating from virtually a thousand different political actors with a cause – and the will to conduct asymmetrical warfare – are spreading havoc throughout the global community. And, again, the deterrence task is straightforward. Culturally effective ways and means must be found to convince these 'non-traditional' players that it is NOT in their interest – whatever it may be – to continue their negative behavior.

Advanced Rules

Success in deterrence cannot be reduced to buying more or better military forces and weaponry, to superior intelligence, to genius in command, or to relative morality. Deterrence can work only if the intended deterree chooses to be deterred. There is no way that any kind of deterrence can be guaranteed. The problem is that deterrence is a dialectic between two independent wills. As a consequence, probably the single most important dimension of deterrence is clarity of communication between deterrer and deterree.

As we rethink contemporary deterrence, we must not think of ourselves as much as 'war fighters' as 'war preventers'. Thus, it is incumbent on the United States and the rest of the global community to understand and cope with the threats imposed by contemporary non-traditional actors, think 'outside the box,' and replace the old 'nuclear theology' with a broad deterrence strategy as it applies to the chaos provoked by the diverse state, non-state, and trans-national nuclear and non-nuclear threats and menaces that have heretofore been ignored or wished away.

What Is To Be Done?

The United States and the rest of the international community will inevitably face horrible new dilemmas at home and abroad that arise from the chaos engendered by the contemporary global security environment. They center on the traditional threat that stems from current and potential nuclear powers, and the many smaller – but equally deadly – non-traditional threats that are generated out of the unevenness of global integration. Clearly, the current 'business as usual' crisis management approach leaves much to be desired in the context of a multipolar world in which one or a hundred 'irrational' political players are exerting differing types and levels of lethal power.

As has been suggested above, the United States needs:

(1) a central unifying deterrence concept to replace 'containment';
(2) a thoughtful reorganization of the national security management, coordination, and implementation structures to better deal with the complex new world; and
(3) farsighted research and planning mechanisms to give decision-makers and policy-makers viable options for deterring, and/or reducing the scope, intensity, and duration of contemporary violence.

Such a prioritization of effort is not a matter of 'putting the strategic cart before the deterrence horse'. It is a matter of making it clear where the horse and cart are going – and how they are going to get there, and what they going to do once they arrive. In that connection, it is important to remember that the intent of these recommendations can only be secured as a result of constant improvements in the types and levels of action we develop in pursuit of a higher quality of global stability and peace than we now enjoy.

This may be accomplished within the context of a holistic implementation of direct and indirect 'offensive' (i.e., proactive preventive diplomacy) and 'defensive' (i.e., generally military) actions. Defensive action involves sustained coercive deterrence of threats to national interests, and, in certain instances, is relatively short term. It primarily involves military and other civilian security efforts that are intended to stop parties in conflict from killing or moving against one another.

Offensive action is generally mid to long term. It is primarily civilian and political-economic-psychological, but is likely to have to be coordinated with defensive military measures. It focuses on prevention of crises, and – when appropriate – follows up the defensive enforcement of law and order with coordinated efforts to diminish or remove the social, economic, and political causes of instability and its resultant violence. This kind of pre or post-crisis action initiates the steps necessary to reform or develop political, economic, and social institutions, procedures, and attitudes that generate the foundational elements required to address America's central strategic vision – that of global engagement to foster legitimate civil society, economic prosperity, and durable peace.

Implementing the extraordinary challenges of reform and regeneration implied in this call for a paradigm change will not be easy. That will, however, be far less demanding and costly in political, military, and monetary terms than continuing a singular crisis management and generally military approach to global security that is inherently a long-term political problem.

Abstracts

Reopening the Deterrence Debate:
Thinking about a Peaceful and Prosperous Tomorrow
Michael P. C. Carns

This introductory article broadens the deterrence debate as it applies to the contemporary global security environment. General Carns argues that as the country that benefits most from global integration, the US has a pressing national interest in maintaining and enhancing the new order. In that connection, the US must learn to understand better and respond more effectively to threats that go beyond nuclear, to chemical and biological, to terrorism, illegal drug-trafficking, organized crime, and to numerous smaller menaces. Finally, he argues that a fresh deterrence policy and strategy framework to replace 'containment' is necessary to manage the evolution of 21st century power relationships.

Deterrence and the Nature of Strategy
Colin S. Gray

This tutorial explores the basics of deterrence. It reconciles deterrence and strategy. And, it explains what deterrence and strategy are, and what they are not. Importantly, Professor Gray also explains the inherent difficulties in applying deterrence and strategy, and cautions those who have equated deterrence with the threat of the use of nuclear weapons. In the end, deterrence is psychological and based on clear, culturally-oriented, and strategically appropriate communications between 'deterer' and 'deteree.' After all, as the author argues, 'with the deterrence mission we seek to influence how and what an enemy thinks'.

Ten Reasons Why Nuclear Deterrence Could Fail:
The Case for Reassessing US Nuclear Policies and Plans
John M. Weinstein

The author argues that serious developments threaten US and global security. The disturbing contemporary reality is that nuclear weapons can neither deter nor provide an appropriate response to all possible threats. At the same time, nuclear deterrence could easily fail as a result of several political, cultural, technological, and bureaucratic reasons. Weinstein also argues that it is time to reassess nuclear policies and plans. The implication is straight-forward – policy-makers should begin that reassessment process by taking cognizance of the reasons why nuclear deterrence could fail.

Some Possible Surprises in Our Nuclear Future
George H. Quester

In this essay, the author makes the argument that current moves to reduce the number of nuclear weapons from their present levels toward zero may well generate some unpleasant surprises. Some surprises may be pleasant, but others might not. That is, the reduction of US and Russian nuclear weapons to zero or near zero could encourage strategic instability and nuclear proliferation elsewhere in the global community. In any case, we really do not have a very good idea about what this new 'non-nuclear' world will be like. We really do not know if there will be pleasant or unpleasant surprises, but there will almost certainly be surprises. One is reminded of the old saying: 'Be careful what you wish for; you may get it.'

The Role of Nuclear Weapons in US Deterrence Strategy
Robert G. Joseph

There are two fundamentals that must be considered in thinking through the deterrent role of nuclear weapons in the contemporary and future security environments. First, there are the countries that represent nuclear threats. Second, there is the question of 'how' US nuclear weapons might deter those discrete threats. Ambassador Joseph makes four conclusions. First, there is a need to retain a nuclear weapons infrastructure that is sufficiently robust to confront actual and potential new adversaries – with new capabilities. Second, the US must not let outdated Cold War concepts and treaties stand in the way of acquiring new deterrence and denial capabilities to ensure national and global security. Third, echoing Professor Quester, the author argues that the US must be more realistic about the likely contributions to security that current arms control proposals can make. Finally, the world has changed fundamentally in the past ten years and will continue to evolve rapidly. Our thinking about who and how to deter must also change.

Deterrence and Conventional Military Forces
Gary L. Guertner

The US must defend and promote its interests in a new environment where threats are both diffuse and uncertain, and where conflict is both inherent and unpredictable. Under these circumstances, US security strategy requires significant departures from Cold War concepts, and new levels of flexibility. In these terms, new conditions require a dramatic and accelerated shift from a nuclear dominant deterrent to one that is based on conventional forces. At the same time, however, the author identifies theories and strategies of nuclear deterrence that can be applied to modern conventional forces in a multi-polar world. There is a caution, however. That is, US deterrence strategy will require a delicate balance between conventional and nuclear forces. Failure to address realistically how and why the US force structure must change will likely result in an impotent mix of forces that will neither deter, nor be capable of meeting a given threat.

Terrorism in the 21st Century:
Reassessing the Emerging Threat
Daniel S. Gressang IV

This is a long but well reasoned analysis of a problem that is not yet well understood. There is a question as to exactly what is terrorism; there is a question of adequate evidence of serious terrorist threats; and there is a question as to whether or not current plans and programs will serve as effective deterrents to possible terrorist threats. Additional questions abound. Suffice it to say here that the possible and probable consequences of terrorist actions can be so catastrophic that the issue can no longer be ignored or wished away – for any reason. Thus, in any effort to craft a preventive or deterrent strategy, knowledge of the adversary is critical. That alone allows for the development of a tailored strategy designed to address the essential elements of contention, or the most significant areas of vulnerability. Nevertheless, the author argues that, in the final analysis, terrorism is a contest of influence more so than it is a contest for power. The most effective deterrence strategy will approach the challenge as such.

Countering Traumatic Attacks
Richard Danzig

In this sobering contribution, Secretary of the Navy Danzig outlines the essentials of new, traumatic attacks on the US and its interests. Dangers for now and the future involve biological and information warfare, chemical and radio-active warfare, and cyber and financial warfare. This is 'non-explosive' warfare. 'Non-explosive' warfare and the traumatic attacks that are manifest in it have grave potential for causing mass social, political, and economic disruption; general panic; and countless physical and non-physical casualties. Finally, the Secretary argues that a line of separation cannot be drawn between 'military' and 'non-military' threats. US and global security depends on civilian utilities, transport, telecommunications, and finance systems that, in turn, depend on healthy and properly functioning civilian information systems and civilian employees. As a result, the US must do two things. First, it must develop programs that will inform and stimulate appropriate defensive and deterrent efforts. Second, it must focus on civilians and civilian systems, as well as on defense, dissuasion, disruption, and deterrence of military operations.

Deterrence and Competitive Strategies:
A New Look at an Old Concept
Robert H. Dorff and Joseph R. Cerami

The authors argue that nuclear deterrence still has much to offer the current security debate. Nevertheless, that debate must return to some basics of deterrence and strategy, and address deterrence in the context of competitive strategies. This is not easy, but the competitive strategies approach helps raise the right questions, to focus on a specific actor and a specific competition, and to consider creative ways to leverage strengths against weaknesses over time. It is also argued that deterrence should entail the use of both 'carrots and sticks'. In that connection, much of what is required for deterrence to be a useful strategic concept is to find an adversary's or potential adversary's 'value inventory' and to leverage it realistically. This is effective in a much broader array of potential relationships than is commonly recognized – including rogue states and their leaders, terrorist organizations and their leaders, and other non-state actors.

The Challenge of Preventive Diplomacy and
Deterrence in the Global Security Environment
Edwin G. Corr and Max G. Manwaring

The US and the rest of the international community will inevitably face horrible new dilemmas at home and abroad that stem from current and potential nuclear powers, and many smaller – but equally deadly – non-traditional threats that are generated out of the unevenness of global integration. Thus, the US faces a challenge to change perspectives. This may be accomplished within the context of a holistic implementation of direct and indirect 'offensive' (i.e., proactive preventive diplomacy) and 'defensive' (i.e., generally military) actions. In turn, that would involve the development of a central unifying field theory of deterrence to replace the theory of containment; a thoughtful reorganization of national security management, coordination, and implementation structures; and farsighted research and planning mechanisms to give decision-makers and policy-makers viable deterrence options as they pertain to the various discrete actors that abound in the world today.

About the Contributors

Prof. **Max G. Manwaring** is Professor of Military Strategy at the US Army War College, a retired Army Colonel and an Adjunct Professor at Dickinson College in Carlisle, PA. He has served at the US Army War College, the Defense Intelligence Agency, and the US Southern Command's Small Wars Operations Research Directorate (SWORD). He has written extensively on political-military affairs. His books include the prize-winning *El Salvador at War*; and *Managing Contemporary Conflict: Pillars of Success* and the forthcoming *The Search for Security: U.S. Grand Strategy for the 21st Century*.

Admiral **William J. Crowe Jr**, USN (Ret.) served as the US Ambassador to the United Kingdom, Chairman of the Joint Chiefs of Staff, and several other military and civilian positions. He is currently the Olin Professor at the US Naval Academy, Chairman of the President's Foreign Intelligence Advisory Board, and on various corporate boards. Admiral Crowe has received numerous US and foreign military and civilian awards and honors, has lectured and written on national security affairs, and is the author of *The Line of Fire*.

General **Michael P. C. Carns**, USAF (Ret.) served as the Vice Chief of Staff of the US Air Force 1991–94. More recently he served as President and Executive Director of the Center for International Political Economy. He is currently engaged in several start-up enterprises and serving on various corporate boards.

Prof. **Colin S. Gray** holds the Chair of International Politics and is the Director of the Centre for Security Studies at the University of Hull, England. He is the author of numerous books on strategy, including *Explorations in Strategy*, and *The Second Nuclear Age*. His most recent book is the highly acclaimed *Modern Strategy*.

Dr **John M. Weinstein** is Chief of the Futures and Initiatives Division of the US Nuclear Command and Control System Support Staff in Washington DC. He has been involved in most aspects of nuclear weapons policy and planning for almost 20 years, and has published numerous articles on the subject in professional journals.

Dr **George H. Quester** is Professor of Government and Politics at the University of Maryland. He is a member of the Council on Foreign Relations, and was a Visiting Professor at the National War College for the 1999–2000 academic year. He is the author of books and articles on international security issues. His latest book *Nuclear Monopoly* addresses American policy in 1945–49.

Ambassador **Robert G. Joseph** (Ret.) is Professor of National Security Studies and Director of the Center for Counter-Proliferation Research at the National Defense University in Washington DC. He has served as the US Commissioner to the Standing Consultative Commission on Nuclear Testing and as the US Representative to the Bilateral Consultative Commission on Nuclear Testing. Amb. Joseph has also held the positions of Principal Deputy Assistant Secretary of Defense for International Security Policy and Deputy Assistant Secretary of Defense for Nuclear Forces and Arms Control Policy.

Dr **Gary L. Guertner** is Dean of Academics at the George C. Marshall Center for Security Studies in Garmisch, Germany. He has also served as Chairman of the Department of National Security and Strategy and as Director of Research at the Strategic Studies Institute of the US Army War College, a staffer at the US Arms Control and Disarmament Agency, and published widely in the field of security policy and nuclear weapons issues.

Mr **Daniel S. Gressang IV** is with the National Security Agency (NSA), is a member of the faculty of the Joint Military Intelligence College (JMIC), and also functions as the NSA/National Cryptologic School Liaison to the JMIC.

Hon. **Richard Danzig** is Secretary of the Navy. He has also served as a Traveling Fellow of the Center for International Political Economy, as Under Secretary of the Navy, and as Principal Deputy Assistant Secretary of Defense for Manpower, Reserve Affairs, and Logistics. Mr Danzig has lectured extensively and written on a variety of national security and legal issues, and have written a book on American and British contract law.

Dr **Robert H. Dorff** is the General Maxwell D. Taylor Chair and Professor of National Security Policy and Strategy at the US Army War College. He is the author and co-author of numerous articles and books dealing with failed and failing states, democratization and global ungovernability, and European and especially German security policy. The results of his research has been published in such professional journals as *Parameters*, *Journal of Politics*, *Publius*, *Comparative Political Studies*, and the *American Political Science Review*.

Colonel **Joseph R. Cerami**, US Army, is Chairman of the Department of National Security and Strategy at the US Army War College. In addition to a distinguished military record in the combat arms, he has taught at the US Military Academy at West Point, and published articles in *Field Artillery*, *Military Review*, and *Parameters*. He is currently serving as Co-Director of a series of workshops on 'Competitive Strategies and Nonproliferation'.

Ambassador **Edwin G. Corr** (Ret.) served as the US Ambassador to Bolivia, Peru, and El Salvador, and as Deputy Assistant Secretary of State for International Narcotics Matters. He is now Director of the Energy Institute of the Americas and Associate Director of the International Programs Center of the University of Oklahoma. Amb. Corr is the recipient of numerous awards and honors, and is co-editor of *Low Intensity Conflict: Old Threats in a New World*.

Index

Note:The Suffix *n* indicates a note after the page on which it appears e.g. 95–6*n*22 means note 22 on pp.95–6